MURDE
& CRIM

HARROGATE
& DISTRICT

CW00460593

MURDER & CRIME

HARROGATE & DISTRICT

JAMES ROGERS

First published 2010

The History Press
The Mill, Brimscombe Port
Stroud, Gloucestershire, GL5 2QG
www.thehistorypress.co.uk

© James Rogers, 2010

The right of James Rogers to be identified as the Author
of this work has been asserted in accordance with the
Copyrights, Designs and Patents Act 1988.

All rights reserved. No part of this book may be reprinted
or reproduced or utilised in any form or by any electronic,
mechanical or other means, now known or hereafter invented,
including photocopying and recording, or in any information
storage or retrieval system, without the permission in writing
from the Publishers.
British Library Cataloguing in Publication Data.
A catalogue record for this book is available from the British Library.

ISBN 978 0 7524 5622 5

Typesetting and origination by The History Press
Printed in Great Britain

CONTENTS

ACKNOWLEDGEMENTS

The spot in Stump's Lane, Darley, where Mary Jane Scaife was murdered in 1858 is supposed to be marked by a cross scratched on a wall. I would like to thank Sue Soroczan for spending a cold and damp October Saturday afternoon walking up and down Stumps Lane with me looking for it. If it is there we never found it. I would also like to thank Sue for her help with some of the photographs.

For the purpose of this book Harrogate and District is defined as an area within an eighteen-mile radius of Harrogate. Information has come from the newspapers of the time; mainly the *Harrogate Advertiser*, the *Leeds Mercury*, the *Leeds Intelligencer*, and the *Yorkshire Gazette*.

One

A BROTHER-IN-LAW POISONED

Arkendale, 1818

Thomas Dodsworth, an Arkendale wheelwright, had two children, a son Joseph and a daughter (whose Christian name is not mentioned in reports of the case). His daughter was married to William Knightson. They all lived in Thomas's house at Arkendale, a small village approximately three miles north-east of Knaresborough and approximately four miles south-west of Boroughbridge. At Christmas 1817 Joseph, who was forty years of age and until then a bachelor, married, and the Knightsons had to move out into a near-by house.

On 25 March 1818 Joseph and William Knightson went to Boroughbridge for some coal. On the way back they called at a public house in Minskip, where they had some beer. On leaving, Knightson produced a penny roll of bread from his pocket, broke a small piece off and gave it to Joseph. Joseph noticed some white substance on the bread, which looked like flour. He mentioned this to Knightson, who said the bread had not been properly baked. Joseph then ate the bread. Soon after, the two parted, Knightson going to Arkendale, Joseph to Knaresborough. Joseph had not gone far when his stomach began to swell and he became violently ill. When he reached Knaresborough he was so ill he had to lie down in a stable and was conveyed part of the way home in a cart. When he arrived home he went straight to bed, where he was visited by Knightson, who appeared much concerned for him, and at the request of Thomas brought him some mint water. When Joseph's wife, Ann, said the mint water looked very thick and muddy, Knightson said he had got it at Mrs Webster's. It was all she had, and she had poured it from the bottom of the container. Knightson told Ann to put some sugar in it and stir it well, but when it was given to Joseph he couldn't keep it down. As a result, Thomas Haws, Thomas's ten-year-old nephew, was sent to Boroughbridge for Mr Sedgwick, the surgeon. Unfortunately, Mr Sedgwick was engaged on another case and couldn't come, but Haws returned with a draught and a large pill, which when given to Joseph appeared to do him some good.

Mr Sedgwick came early the next morning and on examining his patient said someone would have to go to Boroughbridge for medicine. Knightson offered to go,

Arkendale, the home of Joseph Dodsworth. This is a view of the main street.

and returned with some pink medicine with about an inch of white powder in the bottom of the bottle. The cork was unsealed. There were also some small powders to be given to Joseph. Knightson said the bottle had to be shaken thoroughly each time before use and two tablespoons had to be given every four hours. Joseph was given the medicine and powders three times and each time his pain and vomiting increased. Later that day some more medicine was brought by a man named Thomas Steel, and when this was taken it gave Joseph some relief.

Knightson returned that evening and asked how Joseph was. Ann said he had been very ill all day after taking the medicine he (Knightson) had brought, and because of this she had not given him anymore. Knightson said she had done wrong and ought to have continued giving him the medicine, changing medicines, he said, always made people worse, and this was the cause of him being very ill.

On the evening of 1 April, Ann prepared some veal broth, intended only for her husband. Knightson came into the kitchen and asked Thomas what was in the pan on the fire. He replied it was broth for Joseph. When Ann retuned to the kitchen she took a candle and on looking into the pan noticed a white scum, which she took off with a spoon, then tasted the broth. It had a bad taste and inflamed her tongue and throat, but she supposed the broth had been contaminated by the spoon being the same one she had used for giving medicine. She put some oatmeal in the broth to thicken it and later, taking a clean spoon, tasted the broth again, only for her mouth to be affected once more. She asked Thomas and John Haw, who were in the kitchen, to taste the broth, which they did. Although all three had tasted less than a spoonful they were sick and suffered stomach pains for some hours. The next day, as a test, a small quantity was given to the cat, which was immediately seized with violent agonies and died soon after.

Ann, now certain her husband had been poisoned, had not given him the broth but had kept it to show to Mr Sedgwick. On his suggestion she took it to Mark Lambert, a druggist at Knaresborough, who confirmed it contained arsenic. The medicine brought by Knightson was also found to contain arsenic.

Knightson in the meantime had fled, but was arrested in Guiseley and brought back to Knaresborough. As he passed through the town he shouted to the crowd, 'I'm not hanged yet.'

In July Knightson appeared at York Assizes charged with maliciously administering a quantity of deadly poison with intent to murder Joseph Dodsworth. In court Joseph, who was unable to stand, and therefore gave his evidence sitting down, said he had enjoyed good health prior to 25 March, when he had been given the bread by Knightson. Mr Sedgwick said he had prescribed a medicine which would not produce a sediment or sickness.

Mark Lambert confirmed that he had sold Knightson the arsenic, but only after a Knaresborough resident, a Mr Gee, had verified Knightson's statement that the arsenic was to be used to kill rats. Knightson's father swore he had asked his son to buy something that would kill rats.

Mrs Webster said the mint water she had sold had been perfectly clear and transparent when she gave it to Knightson.

There was no known motive for the crime, but it was said Knightson's wife would have inherited a small amount of property on her brother Joseph's death. When Joseph married it was thought the prospect of him now producing children to inherit the property had induced Knightson to act. The jury was out half an hour and on their return found Knightson guilty. He was sentenced to death. There are, however, no newspaper reports that the sentence was carried out and it is possible he was transported for life.

Joseph appears to have made a full recovery, for the 1841 census shows him living in Arkendale with his wife Ann and fifteen-year-old daughter, Elizabeth.

TWO

BROTHER KILLS BROTHER

White Houses, near Pateley Bridge, 1821

White Houses is a small village about two miles from Pateley Bridge. In 1821 Mrs Mason, a widow, ran a butcher's shop there, with the help of two of her sons. On going into the shop on 5 January that year she found her eldest son, Ibbotson Mason, lying dead on the floor, his skull dreadfully fractured and his brains scattered in all directions. A bloody axe lay near the body.

Suspicion fell on one of Mrs Mason's other sons, Joseph, who had been assisting the deceased that morning in dressing a sheep for Pateley Bridge market, and had left the shop just before his mother entered, saying he was going to see his other brother in Knaresborough. A constable was at once sent to that town and arrested him there. When taken prisoner, a butcher's knife was found concealed on his person. At his trial he was found not guilty of murder on the grounds of insanity and was ordered to be detained.

Three

THE DISAPPEARANCE
OF MARY GILL

Belmont, near Knaresborough, 1823

Today Belmont Wood, between Starbeck and Knaresborough, is surrounded by a golf course and is close to the Harrogate-Knaresborough railway line. In 1822 neither the golf course nor the railway existed, and the wood was much larger. On the edge of the wood stood Belmont House (called Belmont Farm in some accounts), the home of Henry Calverley, a farmer, aged about fifty. Also living there were Calverley's wife and six children, and an unmarried servant girl, Mary Gill, aged about thirty. In September 1822 Mary left Calverley's employment and went to lodge with a Betty Leeming in Knaresborough, about a mile away. Mary was pregnant with Calverley's child and later that year, or early the next, gave birth to a daughter, who she named Sarah. Calverley agreed to pay Mary 2s 6d per week maintenance, but she appears to have been dissatisfied with this amount. On 4 October 1823, as was their custom, they met in Belmont Wood and Calverley persuaded Mary to let him have the child, saying he had arranged for a nurse to look after it. As soon as Mary handed him the child, and a clean bundle of the child's clothing, Calverley ran off, leaving her alone in the wood.

Later Mary began to regret handing over her daughter and asked for her return. Calverley told her he had sent the child to Leeds, and, if she wished, she could go and see her. Consequently she arranged for a man to take her to Leeds on his wagon, but later cancelled the arrangement because, she said, Calverley had offered to take her himself. On 8 October she left her lodgings to go to Leeds with Calverley. A few days later a letter, bearing a Leeds postmark, and supposedly written by her, was received by her father, who lived at Great Ouseburn. In the letter she told her father that she had got a place at Leeds, the child was being well taken care of, and she would visit him at Christmas.

When Christmas came and went and the promised visit was not made, suspicion began to be aroused that Calverley had murdered both Mary and her child. Calverley was said to have been in Leeds the day the letter was posted and paper similar to that on which the letter had been written was found in his house. The handwriting was

WHEREAS MARY GILL, who lived Servant with HENRY CALVERLEY, of Belmont-House, near Knaresbrough, in March, 1822, and who was removed by an Order of Two Justices to her Settlement at Wilstrop, near Skipbridge, in the Ainsty of the City of York, the latter end of September following; and whereas it is supposed the said Mary Gill went to reside at Leeds, or in the Neighbourhood, in October 1822, and did bring along with her a Female Child, then about a Year old, which she intended to put out to nurse there; and whereas also it appears the said Mary Gill very soon afterwards wrote or got some Person to write a Letter to John Gill, her Father, at Little Ousebourne, which Letter bears the Leeds Post Mark, and states that she had then got a good Place, and was doing well, and had put the said Child out to nurse, and would return home with it about Christmas following. Now as the said Mary Gill did not return home at the time appointed with the Child, and hath not been heard of ever since, and as both her and the Child's Residence are at this Time particularly wanted to be known and ascertained. Any person therefore giving information where the said Mary Gill or her Child may be met with, or can produce them, or either of them, or give Information who wrote the said Letter directed to the said John Gill, to the Chief Constable of Leeds, or to Mr. Baines, at the Mercury Office, will receive a REWARD of FIVE GUINEAS.

10th January, 1824.

Left: An advertisement from the *Leeds Mercury* of 17 January 1824 offering a reward of five guineas for information leading to the discovery of Mary's Gill's whereabouts.

Below: Belmont House (the home of Henry Calverley) no longer exists, and much of Belmont wood is now occupied by a golf course.

also said to be his. On 9 October a bundle of child's clothing, hidden in a haystack, but pulled out by pigs, had been found by a man named Nelson, who was thatching a haystack near Calverley's house. These were said to be the same clothes that Mary had given to Calverley when she handed the child over to him.

Calverley denied having anything to do with Mary's disappearance. Two people, John Teale and Faith Stephenson, stated that they had seen her after she went missing.

Teale, who was Calverley's husbandry servant, at first refused to answer the magistrates' questions, until they threatened him with imprisonment in York Castle. He said he had seen Mary in Harrogate about a month after she went missing. His manner in giving evidence, however, made the magistrates doubt the truth of his statement, and, on threatening him with a charge of perjury, he confessed his statement was false and that Calverley had said he would make it worth his while if he made it.

Faith Stephenson, fainted whilst being questioned and on recovering said she was not sure the person she had seen was Mary Gill, but Calverley and his wife had told her to swear it was.

Calverley was arrested and charged with the wilful murder of Mary Gill and her child, Sarah Gill. He denied seeing Mary after she left his employment, and said he never had any improper connection with her.

The prison at Knaresborough was not considered secure enough for prisoners detained on criminal charges. Calverley was therefore taken to York Castle in a post chaise, accompanied by two constables. His departure was watched by a large crowd.

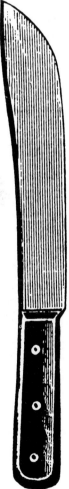

In the meantime, the search for Mary continued. A large body of people searched Belmont Wood. All they found was a carving knife, but there was no evidence to show to whom it belonged. Advertisements were placed in the Leeds newspapers offering a reward of five guineas (£5 5s) to anyone who could say where she could be found, or who had written the letter supposedly written by her. She was said to be a low, broad-set woman, about thirty years of age with a long face and very much marked with the smallpox. When she left Knaresborough she was wearing a brown pelisse with a cape, a black willow bonnet, lined with pink calico, a light brown cotton gown with a yellow star, black leather shoes, tied with a black ribbon, and a black and yellow silk handkerchief tied around her neck. She was carrying an umbrella and a small bundle containing a child's grey cloak, a white Irish apron and a child's frock.

By 4 March 1824 the search for Mary Gill and her daughter had been given up as hopeless, and the feeling in Knaresborough was that the bodies had been burnt.

When Henry Calverley appeared in court on 27 March 1824 the Grand Jury threw out the bill and he was discharged a free man. The fate of Mary Gill and her daughter Sarah remains unknown.

Four

THE DISAPPEARANCE OF JAMES PRIGG

Ribston, 1824

Mary Gill's disappearance wasn't the only one puzzling Knaresborough people in 1824. On 23 January that year James Prigg, a Knaresborough gardener and nurseryman, went with two companions to Kirk Deighton, near Wetherby, to meet John Richardson, an unemployed servant from Leeds, who owed Prigg £25. On arriving at Kirk Deighton Prigg realised he had got the date wrong and the meeting was not due to take place until the following day. The next day Prigg went alone to Kirk Deighton, met Richardson and received the £25 from him. On the return journey to Knaresborough two evil-looking men, who were said to have seen the money handed over, passed Prigg on the highway and jostled him. Suspecting they intended to rob him, Prigg took refuge in a public house at Ribston. Whilst there he mentioned his fears to the landlady and gave her a detailed description of the two men. He told her he would await the return of a friend who had gone to Ribston Hall, and travel with him to Knaresborough. By 8 o'clock (some accounts say 9 o'clock) his friend had not returned. Prigg therefore set out to travel the three miles to Knaresborough alone, along a dark country road, which one report described as running mainly through a wood with no houses within earshot. Prigg was never seen again.

His sister, who kept house for him, was, at first, unconcerned about his absence because he was in the habit of visiting a young woman in Wakefield, and she though he had gone there for a few days. However, by the beginning of February it was commonly believed that he had been murdered by the two men who had passed him on the road and his body hidden in the wood, or thrown into the River Nidd, which flowed alongside part of the road. On the 28 January a pocketbook containing Prigg's name had been picked up in the wood adjoining the road, about half a mile from Ribston, but the finder, not knowing anyone of that name, had, at first, not mentioned it. The pocketbook contained a letter and a receipt for £25. Later, a handkerchief with Prigg's name on it, which he wore around his neck, and a gardener's knife, known to have belonged to Prigg, were found near the same spot. As a result, the constables of Knaresborough, Ribston and Kirk

A map from *Thorpe's Illustrated Guide to Harrogate* (published in 1891) showing the road between Kirk Deighton and Knaresborough on which Prigg vanished. Note how at two points the road runs alongside the River Nidd.

Deighton made a thorough search for his body. The River Nidd was dragged, and the wood through which the road ran explored, but without success.

Opinion in Knaresborough was divided as to whether Prigg had been murdered or had faked his own murder in order to start a new life elsewhere. Memory was still fresh of a man from Thorp Arch Mills, who, on returning from York market, had thrown his pocketbook onto the road, turned his horse loose and disturbed the ground to make it appear a struggle had taken place, and that he had been murdered by highway robbers. A wide search had been made and an industrious farmer at Acomb, near York, had had a field of corn trampled underfoot and destroyed by the searchers. It was later discovered that the 'murdered' man had fled to America to escape his creditors, leaving his wife and family in distress.

A modern-day view of the road from Ribston to Knaresborough on which Prigg vanished.

A Knaresborough solicitor, J.M. Allen, clearly believed Prigg had faked his own murder. He wrote to the *Leeds Mercury* pointing out inaccuracies in their reports. The wood was not as large as they made out; it did not extend above 800 yards. Also there were four houses situated close by whose inhabitants would probably have heard any cries of murder. Allen said he had seen Prigg's pocketbook, and the letter supposedly sent by Richardson to Prigg in which he asked him to meet him at Kirk Deighton. This letter had been found in a trouser pocket by Prigg's sister. In Allen's opinion the handwriting in the pocketbook and on the letter was the same. Prigg, said Allen, had taken a garden for twenty years at an enormous rent and had asked a relation for a loan. In his opinion Prigg, in embarrassed circumstances, and engaged in a ruinous undertaking, had faked his own murder and fled to another part of the country, or even abroad.

Prigg was defended by another, unnamed, correspondent. He said Prigg was twenty-three years of age, unmarried and surrounded by friends. The man from Thorp Arch Mills had thrown his pocketbook in the road, where it could easily be found, but the pocketbook of Prigg had been discovered only by mere accident in the wood. The fact his body had not been found in the River Nidd did not mean it had not been thrown in. The river bed was rocky and subterraneous and a body could remain undiscovered for months. In his opinion Prigg had been murdered by a gang that infested the neighbourhood.

Knaresborough was full of rumours; it was reported suspicion had fallen on a man who lived in a neighbouring village, and who was supposed to be connected to a gang of poachers and game dealers in Knaresborough. He was said to have been aware Prigg had some money to receive from Richardson, and was known to have left his home on the evening of Prigg's disappearance. Another rumour had Prigg on his way to America, and his name entered in a shipping company's books at Liverpool as having taken a passage. However, when the constables wrote to Liverpool they were informed this was not so.

Surprisingly there are no reports of any attempt to trace John Richardson to ascertain if he really existed. Whatever the truth, the story went cold and Prigg appears never to have been found, dead or alive.

Five

A WIFE POISONED

Pannal, 1829

Mary Coates, it was said, had married against her parents' wishes and after only ten months the marriage proved to be an unhappy one, despite the couple having a child. Reports do not mention the name of the village where they lived, but, as they worshiped at Pannal church and she was buried in the churchyard there, it may be assumed they lived in Pannal, or its immediate neighbourhood. Reports do not give the Christian name of Mr Coates, who was a labouring man who worked for a butcher named Wilkinson in Harrogate.

Despite the closeness of their home, Coates remained in Harrogate during the week and only came home on Saturday evenings, spent Sunday at home, then returned to Harrogate. Mary was in perfect health until one Sunday in June 1829 when she was violently sick after eating part of a gooseberry pie she had made. This, together with other symptoms, resulted in her parents, Mr and Mrs Swales, who lived about a mile away, being called to look after her. Despite their attentions, she died the next day. Her parents had brought with them their two small children, Richard and Jane. Before returning home Mr Swales, Richard and Jane ate some of the gooseberry pie. Richard soon complained of a burning pain and of something in his throat, and, on reaching home, was given some milk to drink. He was violently sick and died two days later.

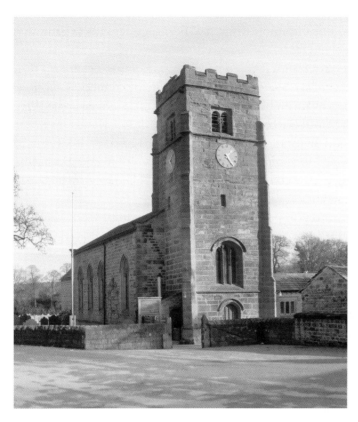

Pannal church, where Coates was arrested after leaving divine service, and where his wife was buried, twice.

Mr Swales and Jane were also violently sick, but eventually recovered. An inquest was held and a verdict that Mary and Richard had died 'By the visitation of God' was returned. This was a common verdict when the cause of death was unknown, but foul play or an accident were not suspected.

On the afternoon of the funeral, Sarah Etty, a neighbour, was in the Coates's house when someone said they had better throw the remains of the gooseberry pie and a cake out, as they were smittled (that is infected by being in the same house as the dead). Etty said she would take them to feed her pigs and chickens, steeped a portion in water and that evening fed it to her chickens. The next morning, on opening the door of the chicken shed, she was amazed to find all the birds (about thirty) dead.

At last people began to suspect that Mary and Richard might have been poisoned. The remains of the pie and cake were recovered from a dung heap, where they had been thrown after the death of the chickens, and were examined by Mr West, an eminent Harrogate chemist. He discovered they contained arsenic. The bodies of some of the dead chickens were opened up and also found to contain arsenic. Orders were given for the bodies of Mary and Richard to be exhumed, and a post-mortem carried out by Mr Thompson and Mr Richardson, surgeons of Harrogate.

The husband of the deceased was the prime suspect and was arrested as he left Pannal church, where his wife had been buried in the churchyard. It was suspicious that his wife had eaten bread made from the same flour as the Gooseberry pie and cake throughout the week before her death and had suffered no ill effects. It was also suspicious that Coates himself had not eaten any of the pie or cake.

However, respectable witnesses came forward and gave evidence that in the past Mary had tried to kill herself by taking harmful substances. A verdict of suicide was therefore returned and Coates was discharged a free man.

Six

A STRANGER MURDERED

South Stainley, 1829

In July 1829 some boys hunting for birds eggs discovered a man apparently asleep in an empty barn near South Stainley, between Harrogate and Ripon. They thought little of it and continued their search for eggs, but later that day mentioned their discovery to

The Red Lion of 1829 no longer exists. This is today's version at South Stainley.

some local men. The men considered a stranger asleep in the barn in the middle of the day suspicious, and suspected that he might be one of a gang of thieves that had been terrorising the neighbourhood. Consequently, they went to the barn and found the man not asleep, but lying in a pool of blood, fatally wounded. An instrument similar to one used by blacksmiths for paring horses' hoofs, and a bludgeon, were found close by. There was a dreadful gash on the man's head, his throat was much swelled and inflamed, as if an attempt had been made to strangle him, and he appeared to have been struck repeatedly with a large stick, or a man's fist. He was at once taken to the Red Lion, and given some cordial. The surgeon at Ripley was sent for, and he did what he could, but despaired of the man's recovery. Before he died the injured man spoke, with some difficulty, and said his name was Joseph Harper, and that he came from Wolverhampton. He also said he had been robbed of 1s 3d.

It was supposed that Harper was connected with the gang of thieves and that he had fallen out with them for some reason, possibly over booty. After an investigation a verdict of wilful murder by some person or persons unknown was returned, but there is no evidence that the murderer (or murderers) was ever caught.

Seven

A CONSTABLE STABBED

Pateley Bridge, 1831

When Thomas Dinsdale, a constable and sergeant at mace at Ripon, went to arrest John and Elisha Sinkler on 18 September 1831 for an aggravated assault on one of Mrs Lawrence's gamekeepers at Studley Park, near Ripon, he was expecting trouble. He therefore took with him three other constables, Sweeting, Binns and Winn. The Sinklers lodged with John Sinkler's father-in-law, a man named Moore, near Pateley Bridge. When Dinsdale knocked on the front door Elisha made his escape via the back door. Sweeting and Binns had foreseen such an eventuality, had positioned themselves there, and arrested him as he left. However, Elisha wasn't one to give up without a struggle and managed to trip Binns up and fall on top of him. In doing so he also brought Sweeting down on top of them both. Dinsdale and Winn then came and managed to handcuff Elisha. They got their prisoner about 150 yards on the road to Pateley Bridge when three woman and two men, John Sinkler and William Longthorne, appeared, armed with bludgeons and knives, determined to rescue Elisha.

John Sinkler and Longthorne took off their coats and produced clasp knives, and ordered the constables to 'Deliver up your prisoner, or we'll stick you.' Longthorne then knocked Dinsdale and Binns down with a bludgeon and threw a large stone at the head of Binns. Fortunately, Winn managed to strike Longthorne's arm with a staff at the vital moment and the stone missed its target. Taking advantage of the struggle Elisha kicked the constables and managed to escape. His brother, John, kicked Dinsdale and cut him severely on both hands and attempted to stab Winn. Several attempts were made to throw Winn over a bridge, his attackers saying they were determined to kill him. They did not succeed but Winn was very much bruised. Dinsdale received several stab wounds. Sweeting suffered much from blows and kicks, but Binns managed to escape without much injury. The affray lasted about half an hour, at the end of which the Sinklers and Longthorne had escaped.

After remaining free for two years Elisha Sinkler and Longthorne were arrested in March 1833 and charged with aiding and abetting John Sinkler, a clock maker of Pateley Bridge, in stabbing Thomas Dinsdale in the execution of his office in serving a warrant on John and Elisha Sinkler on Sunday, 18 September 1831, the day of Pateley Bridge Feast. Elisha said he was quite innocent of the action, while Longthorne declared he, himself, was as innocent as a child unborn of ever having committed such an action. The jury disagreed and found both men guilty. The judge then sentenced both men to be hanged, but they were later reprieved and transported for life.

After being transported Elisha managed to escape and made his way back to England, and by 1843 was once again a notorious poacher and the terror of the Pateley Bridge area. In February that year Thomas Robinson, a gamekeeper employed by John Yorke of Bewerley Hall, was on his rounds with another man when he discovered Elisha hiding in the bottom of a hedge. On being found Elisha attempted to run away but soon turned, and having a gun in one hand, and a pistol in the other, threatened to shoot the first man that came near. Robinson, who had a gun in one hand, and a stout stick in the other, quickly brushed Elisha's arm aside and felled him with one blow of the stout sick. He then shot Elisha's dog.

Elisha later appeared in court charged with having, on 21 February, at Fountains Earth, presented a loaded pistol against Thomas Robinson with the intent to murder him. No evidence was presented and the jury consequently returned a verdict of not guilty. He was also charged with having unlawfully returned from transportation for life. On this charge he was found guilty and sentenced to a month in prison, after which he was again transported for life.

John Sinkler also known as John Hebden, was also arrested in 1843 and charged with having, on 18 September 1831, at Pateley Bridge, stabbed, cut and wounded Thomas Dinsdale with intent to do him some grievous bodily harm. He was found guilty and the death sentence was recorded against him. This appears not to have been carried out, and it seems likely he too was transported for life.

Eight

THE COLLINGHAM GHOST

Collingham, 1834

The villagers of Collingham, near Wetherby, were terrified in February 1834, so much so that they dared not leave their homes after dark. As night fell unearthly moans and groans could be heard, but nothing seen. The noises began in a wood on the brow of a hill between their village and Thorp Arch, and moved across fields to the brook which ran parallel to the Wetherby Road. After about two hours the noises retreated back to the wood. A blacksmith, who had also been a notorious poacher, had died in the village not long before, and because the moans and groans had begun on the night of his funeral residents of Collingham and neighbouring villages were convinced it was his ghost which made the unearthly sounds. It was said bloodhounds sent into the wood had returned with their tails between their legs. Also any traveller who dared venture out after dark on the turnpike road could travel for free because the toll gate keepers, who heard the moans and groans regularly, were too frightened to leave their houses to collect the tolls.

Not everyone, however, was frightened and large groups came from all parts to roam the lanes at night in an attempt to see the ghost. Five men from nearby Boston Spa decided to trap the ghost. They formed themselves into a large circle, but when they heard the moans and groans, they saw nothing and their courage deserted them and they ran as fast as their legs could carry them back to Boston Spa, where they reported the terrifying event.

Such was the fear the sounds produced in the local population the magistrates began to take an interest. The result was that in March a man was arrested after being found at night hiding under a bridge with a speaking trumpet. His job had been to make the moans and groans to frighten off the gamekeepers and others, whilst his friends went about their poaching activities.

That would appear to have been that, but a year later, in January 1835, the *Leeds Intelligencer* reported that the ghost had not yet been discovered, and a voice coming from no one knows where was again heard each night. One night three gentlemen travelling from Leeds to Wetherby were about a mile from Collingham Bridge when they heard close to them what they considered to be a human voice say, 'Bob, Bob,' an expression said to be used by the ghost. Thinking someone was hiding behind the hedge, one of the men dug his spurs into his horse and jumped the hedge, but found no one there. Then to his astonishment he, and his companions, heard the same cry of 'Bob, Bob' coming from about half a mile away.

Nine

A HUSBAND POISONED

Dallowgill, 1834

On 6 November 1834 William Lofthouse, a clogger, of Dallowgill, a small village in the parish of Kirby Malzeard, near Ripon, went to Ripon market with his sister-in-law, the wife of his brother Henry (reports do not give her Christian name). At Ripon the pair had about two pints of beer and, on returning to his sister-in-law's house at Dallowgill, William had a pint of fresh milk and some bread, smoked a pipe, and at about 7 o'clock went home. About half an hour later William's wife, Ursula, called on Henry much distressed and said William was very ill and likely to die. Henry went to see him at once and found him vomiting and racked with pain. William at first declined to have the doctor called out, because he had been ill before and had recovered. However, the following morning, when he was no better, he relented. Dr Storey came and found him complaining of pains in the stomach and bowels, having no perceptible pulse, spasmodic pain in the left arm, an intolerable thirst and suppression of urine, the pupils of the eyes projecting and the blood vessels of the eye turgid. From these symptoms the doctor, who had been in practise twenty years, concluded his patient was suffering from cholera. He therefore proscribed opium, ether and rhubarb. This did no good and William died at 2 o'clock the following afternoon. He was buried the next day, Sunday.

Suspicion that William might have been poisoned arose after some hens kept by him died suddenly. It was found that Ursula had purchased some arsenic, and had baked a cake. She later admitted her husband had eaten nearly the whole of the cake, after which he had said he would not eat another bit for the whole of the world, and, on getting up for his pipe, had staggered and fallen down. William's body was exhumed and the contents of the stomach examined by Dr West, a chemist from Leeds, who discovered the presence of white arsenic therein. He also found arsenic in the bodies of two of the hens that had died. Ursula was arrested and charged with the wilful murder of her husband.

In April 1835 she appeared at York Assizes. She was twenty-six years of age and described as a decent-looking woman with a Jewish stature. She was dressed in mourning clothes. Reports do not give any reasons why she should want to murder her husband, nor how long they had been married. She pleaded not guilty, saying, 'I have nothing to say Sir, but I am innocent.' The jury, however, did not think so and after twenty minutes' deliberation returned a verdict of guilty. The judge then sentenced her to be hanged the following Monday. At this she wept profusely and when removed from the bar was quite insensible.

She was hanged on Monday, 6 April 1835 at York Castle, with two other murderers, William Allot and Joseph Heeley. It was the first triple hanging in Yorkshire for some time. The scaffold had been erected in the castle garden, and, as it was a public execution, a large crowd had gathered. The prisoners were afforded some dignity and were allowed to stand with their backs to the crowd. All three had devoted some time to prayer, assisted by the prison chaplain, Revd Flower. Ursula protested her innocence, saying her husband had told her to buy the arsenic and had drunk some in his tea. He had threatened that if she gave the alarm he would say she had poisoned him. However, it was said she later tacitly admitted her guilt. She was still dressed in her mourning clothes with a red spotted handkerchief round her neck. She used another handkerchief to cover her face. She was placed between the two male prisoners and shortly after noon all three were launched into eternity. After hanging the usual hour the bodies were cut down and buried within the walls of the castle.

Ten

THE DEATH OF A
CLIMBING BOY

Near Harewood, 1836

In Victorian times almost all houses were heated by an open fire, burning either coal or wood. Chimneys often did not go straight up and had ledges and corners where soot would accumulate. Because brushes could not reach these ledges and corners, small boys were used to climb the inside of the chimney and scrape and brush away the soot. Needless to say this was unpleasant and dangerous work. One such climbing boy was Michael Hurley. He had been apprenticed to a Mrs Haigh, a mistress chimney sweep, at Leeds when only seven years old. When he was eleven he ran away. On his travels he met another sweep, a Mr Taylor, and went to live with him at Ripon. A few weeks later, in February 1836, news of his whereabouts reached Mrs Haigh, who sent one of her journeymen, a man named George Gidley, to fetch him back. On his way to Ripon, Gidley was heard to say what he would do to Michael when he caught him.

Having caught him, the two set off from Ripon at eight in the morning for Leeds (which was approximately thirty miles away) on foot. Taylor said later that Michael had a good breakfast before they left and was in good health. Mrs Haigh had given Gidley 5s for refreshments on the road for both himself and Michael, but Gidley spent all of it on himself. At Harrogate Gidley drank five pints of beer and ate some bread and bacon, after which he continued the journey to Leeds, driving the boy before him with a heavy stick. At Harewood bridge Gidley went into Mr Scott's public house and called for a noggin of gin. One of Lord Harewood's gamekeepers noticed that Michael looked exhausted, took him into the kitchen and sat him down in front of the fire. He offered him some gin but Michael declined to take it. He appeared weak and too exhausted to eat or drink, but Gidley said he was putting in on. Those in Mr Scott's accepted this, much to their later regret.

Between eight and nine that evening the journey towards Leeds was resumed, with Gidley now the worse for drink. Ascending the hill to Harewood village Michael's strength seemed to desert him, but Gidley continued to beat him onwards. A woman at

Harewood Bridge, where Gidley stopped for refreshments. Mr Scott's public house is unfortunately long gone.

Harewood village, on hearing the blows, assumed a donkey or mule was being beaten and was horrified to see the blows were being received by a young boy. She cried out, 'Oh, you'll kill that boy,' but Gidley made a light remark and moved on, urging the boy on with further blows. As they left the village Michael begged for water, only to be denied by Gidley, with the remark, 'I'll give you plenty of water by and by.'

At Wike Lane end, about one and a half miles from Harewood, Michael collapsed, only for Gidley to strike him again. Gidley later claimed he had carried the boy two miles towards Leeds, where they sought shelter in a shed. Being February it was now dark and frosty. The shed was open to the elements on three sides and consequently did not provide much shelter. At two in the morning Gidley awoke and found Michael dead. He then went to the house of Mr Pickersgill, a farmer at Alwoodley, awoke him and told him he had a boy with him who had died. Several people then went to the shed with a light and found the boy so stiff and cold they considered he must have died some hours before.

An inquest was later held. The body had been examined by Mr Ward of Leeds and Mr Hirst of Chapel Allerton, both surgeons. Despite their evidence that Michael's body showed signs of a severe beating, a verdict of 'died from starvation' was returned.

Wike Lane end, where Michael collapsed. Harewood House can be seen in the distance.

When news of the verdict reached Harewood the villagers were outraged, and there was much talk in the village, talk which reached the ears of Lord Harewood. His Lordship ordered an immediate investigation, an investigation in which his two sons took an active part. Michael's body was exhumed and taken to Leeds, where it was examined by two surgeons, Mr Hey and Mr Garrick. They found the boy's stomach empty, except for some green matter, which was supposed to have been leaves or other vegetable substance. They also found the body covered with bruises. Gidley, who had been discharged by the coroner's verdict, was now arrested and charged with murder. He admitted driving Michael before him, but claimed that the boy had refused refreshment when it was offered. He was supported in this by Sarah Clarkson of the Brewer's Arms, Harrogate, who said Gidley had three times offered the boy something to eat, which he refused, and seemed sulky. Gidley said he had beaten Michael because he considered him obstinate, not weak. It was believed Michael had died whilst being beaten at Wike Lane end and Gidley had carried the body two miles to the shed to make it appear he had died in the night. The cudgel used to beat Michael had disappeared, but after a diligent search a portion of it, recently broken, was found between Wike Lane end and the shed. Mrs Haigh declared she always treated Michael

Knaresborough Court House, where the chimney was illegally swept in 1864.

well and thought him a good boy who always worked willingly. She also said Gidley was fond of him. However, on another occasion she said Michael had run away a number of times and she considered him to be of a sullen and stupid disposition.

Gidley was found not guilty of murder, but guilty of manslaughter, and was sentenced to twelve months imprisonment with hard labour in the Wakefield House of Correction.

The *Leeds Intelligencer* remarked that the case should induce all humane persons to determine to discourage chimney sweeping by means of the human instrument when the inanimate machine is found to be equally effective in nine cases out of ten.

In 1840 an Act of Parliament forbade anyone under the age of 21 climbing a chimney, but because the penalties were small it was largely ignored. Another Act of 1864 was also largely ignored. In that year John Lowther of Knaresborough was summoned for a breach of the Chimney Sweepers Act in allowing a boy to sweep a chimney. Despite Lowther having a blatant disregard for the law, it was the Court House chimney that had been swept, the case was dismissed and the West Riding surveyor was instructed to have the court house chimneys properly constructed forthwith.

Finally, in 1875, an Act required all chimney sweeps to be licensed and licenses were only issued to those sweeps who did not employ climbing boys. This brought the employment of climbing boys to an end.

Eleven

CHILDREN MURDERED BY THEIR FATHER

Ripon, 1837

On the evening of 15 June 1837 William Marshall, a thirty-five-year-old shoemaker, who lived in Skellgate, Ripon, filled two large wooden tubs with water. He threw some marbles in one and then called his son, aged about seven, in from play and asked him to take them out. As the child leaned into the tub to reach them Marshall held the child's head under water until life was extinct. He then took his other child, an eleven-month-old baby, and drowned it in the other tub. He then undressed them both and put them to bed. His wife was out working as a charwoman at the time. Needless to say she was distraught when she returned home and discovered what her husband had done. Marshall was arrested but found not guilty of murder on the grounds of insanity. He had not previously shown any signs of metal derangement.

Part of Skellgate Ripon, where two small children were murdered by their father.

Twelve

NEIGHBOURHOOD WATCH

Knaresborough, 1840

In an early example of Neighbourhood Watch the *Leeds Intelligencer* reported in April 1840 that, in addition to the paid watchmen, up to a dozen of the respectable inhabitants of Knaresborough, mainly tradesmen, had commenced watching the town, and the roads leading to it, each night for the purpose of protecting the town from the lawless banditti of burglars which infested the district.

Thirteen

A KNIFE FIGHT

Ripon, 1840

In October 1840 a quarrel broke out amongst some young men in a public house in Westgate, Ripon. The landlord ordered them out and the quarrel turned into a fight in the yard behind the pub. One of the men, John Meldrum, stabbed another, Alfred Wells. Wells ran after him but soon became weak from loss of blood. He was conveyed home, where he was attended by Mr Bruce, a surgeon. Meldrum quickly left the neighbourhood. The *Leeds Intelligencer* considered it was time a stop was put to this vile and un-English propensity. No less than three of the young men involved in the fight had had knives drawn and threatened anyone who dared interfere with them. If this evil was not checked, the *Leeds Intelligencer* believed, the stiletto and poniard (types of knives) would soon be as fashionable amongst the English as they were in Italy and Spain.

Fourteen

THE MURDER OF THE LANDLORD OF THE WHITE HART

Knaresborough, 1841

In Knaresborough market place there stood, in 1841, a small public house, the White Hart (called the Old White Hart in some accounts). The landlord was Joseph Cocker, a widower aged fifty-six, who lived alone. On the evening of 16 June 1841 three Knaresborough men, John Burlinson (twenty-four) Henry Nuttall (twenty-two) and Charles Gill (nineteen) went for a drink at the White Hart, but their real intention was robbery. Their plan was foiled when Nuttall's employer, William Inchboard, a Knaresborough tallow chandler, came in. Undaunted they returned the following night at about half past ten and had five pints of ale. At about midnight Cocker refused to let them have anymore, and told them they had better be going home as it was late. In reply Burlinson struck Cocker on the head with a hammer. Cocker at once fell to his knees and said, 'Oh lads don't murder me.'

The Market Place, Knaresborough, looking towards the 'synagogues'.

Cocker's next-door neighbour was Charles Snow, a shoemaker. Snow's wife, hearing some groaning and a sound as if someone was beating an animal, went into her yard to investigate. Using an upturned bucket she climbed on to what she called her ash place, and looked through Cocker's kitchen window. She could not see him, but saw three men she did not recognise, and heard one say, 'Let us take him to the cellar.' Climbing down from the upturned bucket she went to Cocker's front door and, on finding it fastened, shook it with all her might and called out, 'Cocker, are they murdering you?'

After hearing Mrs Snow, Nuttall ran off, but the other two went after him and brought him back. Gill then struck Cocker, who was lying in the fireplace, four or five times with the hammer.

In the meantime Mrs Snow had returned home and woken her husband, who had gone to bed an hour before. She urged him to be quick as she thought some men were killing Cocker. She returned to the yard and once again used the upturned bucket to climb on to her ash place. Looking through the kitchen window she saw Cocker reared up against the chimney piece, groaning heavily, but she could not distinguish a word he said. She noticed the floor where he was stood was covered with blood. Mrs Snow then returned home and once again urged her husband to be quick. They went into the yard and Mrs Snow climbed onto her ash place and looked through the kitchen window. She saw the same three men in the house again. Cocker was lying across the floor with one man kneeling down, apparently rifling through Cocker's pockets. She then got down to let her husband take a look. Mr Snow recognised the men as Knaresborough men, but did not know their names. One (Burlinson) lived with his widowed mother, perhaps eight or nine doors from Snow, and used to work at a mill. Another's (Gill) father-in-law, George Ingle, kept a pleasure boat on the river.

While Snow was looking through the window the men left the house. They ran across the street and up the Synagogues (a passage that led from the market place). Two then went down a back street and one ran up Jockey Lane into the High Street. They afterwards met on the High Bridge, which carries the main Knaresborough-Harrogate road over the river, and then went into Dunmore's fields towards Bilton Woods, where Nuttall threw the hammer into the river at a place called Cherry Tree Deep, about 200 yards above the High Bridge. They then returned separately to the town.

Mr Snow now realised the seriousness of the situation and returned to his house for a pistol. He then went to awaken David Vickerman, a police officer, and raised the alarm with the neighbours.

The White Hart's front door now opened easily and, on entering, Vickerman and the Snows heard groaning in the darkness. On lighting a candle they found Cocker lying face down on the floor in a pool of blood with a poker partly across his legs and partly across the fender. A chair and the white-washed walls of the kitchen were covered in blood. Vickerman removed the poker and turned Cocker face up. Cocker had a number of serious head wounds, was insensible and could not answer questions put to him. Vickerman found the injured man's breaches' pockets were turned inside out and

Above: Jockey Lane, Knaresborough, down which one of the murders ran after killing Cocker. The view is towards the High Street.

Right: Cherry Tree Deep, into which the murder weapon was thrown. Is it still down there?

had nothing left in them. After wiping the blood from Cocker's face and mouth with a handkerchief, which he found on the floor, he asked Mr Snow to hold Cocker's head whilst he ran for Thomas Beaumont, the surgeon. Beaumont, unfortunately, could do little to help Cocker, who died shortly after his arrival.

Vickerman then went for the other town constables, Joseph Dixon and John Brotherton, also a number of the inhabitants. Dixon and Brotherton appear to have been part-time constables because Dixon was later described in court as a grocer, and Brotherton as a plumber and glazier. Vickerman told the Knaresborough inhabitants he had gathered to go in different directions and apprehend anyone who could not give a good account of themselves.

Burlinson was apprehended by Constable Brotherton at around 1 a.m. He was being held by a man Brotherton did not know in the street about 20 yards from Cocker's house. Burlinson asked if they had caught Nuttall and remarked if the constables had run a little quicker down the back street they would have caught him.

Gill was apprehended by Constable Dixon near the old cotton mill wall corner, near the riverside, in a very solitary place, about 150 years from where he lived. Dixon did not have a watch but estimated the time to be about 1.30 a.m.

Dixon later arrested Nuttall in Bond End, and, on taking him to the court house, found on him 3s 6d in silver and 2s 5¾d in copper. On Gill he had found 1s 1½d. It was later thought that thanks to the Snows the murderers had had no time to ransack the house because a pocketbook containing £6 was found upstairs.

Vickerman had taken the Harrogate road but was soon overtaken by a man on horseback and told three men had been taken. He consequently returned home and found the three men in the prison he kept. The clothes of all three were heavily bloodstained, as was Burlinson's face and hands. All three were cautioned and told that anything they said might be given in evidence and they were not obliged to say anything. They were then asked how they had got into such a state. Burlinson gave no answer, and Gill said he had had a nose bleed. Vickerman then proceeded to strip the men naked so that their clothes could be used as evidence.

At their trial at York Crown Court in July 1841 all three pleaded not guilty. Nuttall claimed he was innocent and nothing had been said beforehand about attacking Cocker. After two or three pints of ale he went in to the yard to 'make water' and when he returned, two or three minutes later, Cocker was down. He was asked to bar the door and did so, but soon opened it and ran away. The other two ran after him. Nuttall claimed he could not have lifted his hand against Cocker. His employer, William Inchboard, said Nuttall had worked for him, on and off, for five or six years and he had never heard anything against him.

Mr Beaumont, the surgeon, however, gave evidence that the poker found at the scene was unlikely to have delivered the fatal blows and Inchboard said that a cooper's adze, one end of which was a hammer, was missing from his premises, and it was thought this might have been the murder weapon.

Burlinson said that they all knew what they were going to do. They were all as willing as the other. The murder weapon belonged to Nuttall. Nuttall had given it to him. It was a long hammer. Burlinson admitted he struck the first blow, with the hammer. Nuttall had barred the door.

In desperation, the defence argued it was probable a quarrel had arisen over the refusal of Cocker to serve the men more drink, and the blows had been given as a consequence. This would reduce the charge of murder to one of manslaughter.

The jury retired for about fifteen minutes and on their return the foreman pronounced a verdict of guilty against all three prisoners. The prisoners were unmoved and when asked if they had anything to say why judgement of death should not be pronounced upon them according to law they gave no answer.

The judge, Mr Justice Wightman, was deeply affected, and, having put on his black cap, the symbol of a death sentence, proceeded to pass sentence. He spoke in such a low and tremulous tone it was difficult for the court to hear what he said. As near as the reporter could make out he said:

John Burlinson, Henry Nuttall and Charles Gill you have been convicted upon the clearest evidence of the crime of murder and by the laws of God and man you must pay the penalty of that offence. For you there is no hope of a pardon in this world. I therefore would earnestly exhort you to seek to obtain that mercy from your heavenly Judge which is in vain for you to expect in this world. The painful duty now only remains for me to pronounce the awful sentence of the law, which sentence is that you, John Burlinson, Henry Nuttall and Charles Gill, be taken from hence to the place from whence you came and that afterwards you, and each of you, be taken from thence to a place of execution and that there you will be hanged by the neck until each of you be dead, and that afterwards your bodies be buried within the precincts of the prison in which you have been confined, and may God in his infinite goodness have mercy on your souls.

The judge then hid his face in his hands, but the prisoners made no sign. After they had been removed from the dock Gill appeared to faint. Nuttall for some time held up his hands as if in supplication and Burlinson laid his head on his left hand, which held a pocket handkerchief. As they were led across the castle yard Nuttall said to one of the constables who had given evidence against him, 'Damn you, you have done your worst, but we shall find heaven a far better place than this.'

Whilst awaiting execution at York the prisoners conducted themselves in a most penitent manner, and were attended by no less than four clergymen. Gill spent most of his time in bed, suffering from erysipelas, a severe skin rash accompanied by fever and vomiting. The night before the execution the men sat up all night, as was the custom, praying. At 5.30 a.m. on Saturday, 7 August 1841 they were removed from their cells to one adjoining the scaffold. Burlinson and Nuttall walked with a firm step but Gill, because of his illness, had to be supported by two attendants. At this time executions were pubic and Saturday was the usual day for execution, because it drew the largest crowd. On the Friday night great numbers of people had travelled on foot from the adjoining towns and villages, especially Knaresborough, and by 11 a.m. a large crowd had assembled in front of the scaffold. This crowd grew even larger as 12 o'clock approached. The prisoners were brought out, and it was said that their demeanour was that of the deepest contrition and penitence. After the usual preliminaries the bolt was drawn and the men were launched into eternity.

Fifteen

A BABY THROWN INTO THE RIVER NIDD

Knaresborough, 1842

On 9 June 1842 Stephen Smith was fishing in the River Nidd near the High Bridge, Knaresborough, when he noticed a bundle, or parcel, floating down the river, out of which protruded a baby's leg. With assistance he managed to bring the bundle to the riverbank, and on opening it found it contained the body of a baby. Mr Powell, surgeon, was called and was of the opinion the child had been born alive, but had died from negligence at the time of birth. He estimated the child had been dead for two or three weeks. Suspicion fell on Jane Elwood, a twenty-one-year-old single girl. She was interviewed by a police officer, David Vickerman, who accused her of recently giving birth to a child. When she denied the allegation, Vickerman threatened to have her examined by a surgeon. She then made a statement to him which satisfied him that his suspicions were well founded. He consequently had her examined by Mr Powell, and she made a further statement to him. As a result, she was arrested and charged with having, on 23 May 1842, at Knaresborough, endeavoured to conceal the birth of a child by throwing it into the River Nidd.

Bilton Fields, Knaresborough, with the High Bridge in the distance.

At Jane's trial Mr Hall, for the defence, said the statement she had made to Vickerman, in which she denied the allegation, was admissible as evidence because it had been made voluntary, but, he argued, the statements she had made to Vickerman and Mr Powell (which were not reported) were inadmissible as evidence because they had been obtained under duress, in that she had been threatened with examination by a surgeon. After some discussion the judge agreed, and, as there was no other evidence against her, the jury, under the Learned Commissioner's direction, found her not guilty.

Sixteen

MURDER ON THE ROAD

The Road from Boroughbridge to Lower Dunsforth, 1844

William Inchbald, a retired merchant of Lower Dunsforth, was a slightly eccentric and wealthy man. He always carried a large wallet under his waistcoat, which he would show to anyone present when he wanted to take any small document from it. He was also in the habit of taking out large amounts of gold and silver when he had to pay for anything, however small the purchase price.

On the morning of Saturday, 28 September 1844 he went on foot to Boroughbridge, approximately three miles away, to attend the market, as was his custom. At 6 o'clock in the evening, quite well and sober, he left the Malt Shovel Inn at Boroughbridge to go home. About a quarter of an hour later he was seen lying by the roadside, about 200 yards from the Aldborough side of Dunsforth Gate by James Topham, who was driving a horse and cart. Topham drove passed thinking Inchbald was asleep, but returned soon after with Inchbald's wife. They then discovered Inchbald, far from being asleep, had been shot and was badly wounded. They took him home and sent for Roger Sedgewick, a surgeon. However, his injuries were severe and he died soon afterwards. Before he died, Inchbald told the surgeon that as he was passing a narrow lane between Aldborough and Lower Dunsforth, opposite a large dung heap, he heard the sound of a gunshot and immediately felt himself shot in the back. He turned round and received a second shot in the left arm. He then saw a man pass him carrying a gun on his shoulder, but could not describe him.

The main suspect was William Kendrew. He was thought to be a stranger to Inchbald and had no business with him, but at noon on the day of the murder he had been at Boroughbridge and had asked a man named Fawcett if he had seen anything of Inchbald that day. Several witnesses came forward to say they had seen Kendrew following Inchbald home from Boroughbridge that evening. Kendrew had apparently hidden a gun in a large dung heap in a field by the roadside. He had overtaken Inchbald on the road, retrieved the gun and waited for him.

One Witness, Robert Horseman, said that at about 6.30 p.m. he was on his way home by Sledbar Nook. Just as he got into the road, he saw Kendrew walking at a very

The Malt Shovel Inn, Boroughbridge, which Inchbald left at 6 p.m.

The village green, Aldborough.

rapid rate towards Dunsforth. He spoke to him but only got some very short answers. He tried to keep up with him but could not as he (Horseman) was carrying a pack of wheat on his back which his wife had been gleaning. A few yards further on he saw Inchbald, who was also walking towards Dunsforth. Kendrew at the time was a few yards behind Inchbald. He then lost sight of them because of a bend in the road. When he got to Bog Lane end, just beyond the bend in the road, he saw Kendrew had got in front of Inchbald. When he turned off the road to go home he heard a gunshot, which seemed to come from between Pick's farmhouse and Lumley's. When he got to his own house he heard two more shots, one after the other, which seemed to come from the neighbourhood of Pick's farmhouse.

Thomas Buck was in a field 286 yards from where the murder was committed. He heard two shots between 6 and 7 o'clock, one quickly after the other, and almost immediately heard cries of someone in distress, apparently proceeding from the place where Inchbald was found. However, he did not investigate and later said he thought nothing serious had occurred.

William Robson was in Lumley's field nearly 800 yards distant, and heard two shots and some person crying out, 'Oh dear' three times in what he described as a very awful manner, but he too did not investigate. Three other witnesses said they heard two shots, one rapidly after the other.

At about 7.30 p.m. Mary Thompson saw Kendrew come down the front street of Aldborough and go into his father's house. He changed his clothes and shoes then went to the Drovers Inn in Boroughbridge where he told his brother-in-law, James

The bridge at Boroughbridge, over which the Kendrews made their escape.

Scott, that he had no bed to sleep in. Scott said he could have half his brother's bed, who was lodging at his house. At about midnight they went out with some nets to fish and came back about 1.30 a.m. Kendrew then remained in bed until 2 p.m. on Sunday afternoon. Scott went out, and, on returning at about 7 p.m., told Kendrew that people were blaming him (Kendrew) for the shooting of Inchbald. Kendrew replied, 'Blaming me?' to which Scott said, 'Yes and if thou art clear thou'll turn out and show thyself like a man, and if thou isn't thou shan't be long in my house' and, being apparently indigent, threw the door wide open and left. Kendrew begged Scott's wife, Jane, to go to a public house called Swales's and inquire if it was true they were looking for him. She returned, said it was true and told him to go clear himself, but he said he would lay 'sulk all night and give himself up in the morning.' That night Kendrew and his brother John were seen crossing the bridge at Boroughbridge by a man named Barlow. Barlow immediately informed the police, who went in pursuit, but in the dark the bothers escaped.

The Kendrews were not seen again until 7 October when a police officer went to the Old Robin Hood Inn in Pilgrim Street, Newcastle, where he found William Kendrew, who gave his name as William Smith, from Leeds. The officer apprehended him on the charge of shooting Inchbald at Boroughbridge, and asked who the man in the other room was. Kendrew said he was called John Palmer, who he had met on the tramp. It was in fact his brother John. (John Palmer was the alias used by the famous highwayman Dick Turpin, hanged at York over 100 years earlier in 1739. Whether this was just coincidence or the reason Kendrew used the name it is not known.)

On being taken back to Boroughbridge John Kendrew asked one of the police officers, 'Who was it that ran after us that night?' meaning the night they had escaped from Boroughbridge. The officer replied, 'It was me and Hutchinson'

'Nay,' said John. 'It wasn't Hutchinson; it was someone that could run faster. It was a rare job you didn't come up with us or you would have catched it.' On saying this, another officer asked if he had a brace of pistols with him that night. 'Nay,' said John, 'I had not a brace, but I would have bitten thee.' It was true John had not a brace of pistols, but he had one he had stolen.

William was charged with the wilful murder of William Inchbald. His brother John, aged twenty-four, was charged with feloniously harbouring and maintaining him knowing him to have committed the murder.

At their trial evidence was given that a week before the murder some young men were on Boroughbridge common shooting bats. One of them had borrowed a gun from a man named Powell. This gun had one nipple larger than the other and required two different sorts of caps. This gun was later stolen and seen in the possession of William. On the day before the murder William was said to have gone into the shop of a man named Buckle and bought some powder, shot and caps. It was claimed that he told Buckle his gun needed caps of different sizes as it had one nipple larger than the other. After the murder the police had found the gun hidden in the thatch of a pigsty at the house of Kendrew's father. They also found, in the pocket of coat owned by William, shot and powder the same as that used in the murder.

Buckle, after looking intently for a few minutes at William, identified him as the man who had bought the shot, but remarked he looked slightly different in court. The man who had bought the shot looked between thirty and forty years of age, William was only twenty-two.

The brothers were undefended in court, something the judge regretted, saying in his summing up they had not had the benefit of some of those zealous, ingenious and well-argued defences which had more than once been heard during the present assizes. They also called no witnesses in their defence. The jury took about fifteen minutes to reach a verdict. William was found guilty and John not guilty. When William was asked why sentence of death should not be passed upon him in due course of law he made no reply. The judge then put on the black cap and sentenced him to be hanged. William then said, 'Thank ye if that be all.' He was then removed from the court.

In prison William showed no remorse and pleaded innocence, but shortly before his execution he made a full confession. He said Inchbald had threatened to have him transported for poaching, and this was the motive for the murder, not robbery. He had followed Inchbald home and when a convenient opportunity had arisen had shot him in the back. Inchbald had then turned round and came at him. He consequently shot him a second time and as he fell to the ground struck him on the head with the butt of his gun before running off across the fields. He also said he had not bought the shot from Buckle himself but had sent a young boy for it. The prison Chaplin, the Revd T. Sutton, read him the text from Revelations 1:7, 'Behold he cometh with clouds and every eye shall see him and all kindred's of the earth shall wail because of him. Even so, Amen.'

William Kendrew was hanged on 28 December 1844. The execution was public and some newspapers printed a report that a pickpocket had been seen at work among the crowd at the foot of the gallows. The *Yorkshire Gazette* said this was untrue. Such stories often appeared after a hanging and were the work of those opposed to the death penalty.

John Kendrew was later charged with stealing a pistol, the property of Ann Glenton. Mrs Glenton was a widow, who, on being thrown on her own resources after the death of her husband, had begun a business as a milliner and dressmaker. To improve herself in her calling she had gone to stay at Harrogate, and let part of her house at Boroughbridge to Kendrew's brother-in-law, James Scott, a shoemaker. John was also a shoemaker and worked for him. On 29 September the door of the room in which the pistol was kept was broken open and the pistol stolen. When John was arrested in Newcastle on 7 October, a pawnbroker's ticket for a pistol, pledged by him a few days before at Sunderland, was found on him. The ticket was taken to the pawnbrokers, the pistol identified as the one stolen and John as the man who had pledged it.

At his trial he offered no defence and the jury immediately found him guilty. His Lordship, in sentencing him, said he could not dismiss altogether from his mind the object for which the pistol was probably stolen and he therefore sentenced him to be transported for seven years. On hearing his sentence John put his hand to his brow, bent his head to the judge and in a firm tone of voice said, 'Thank you my lord,' and then leapt down into the dock apparently quite elated.

Seventeen

SUSPECTED BURGLAR SHOT

Near Beckwithshaw, 1846

One Saturday night in January 1846 a young Beckwithshaw man named Brotherton went secretly late at night to the house of Mr Atkinson, a respectable farmer, who lived at a farm called Briska Ridge, situated about three or four miles from Harrogate on the road to Otley. His intention was to wake his girlfriend, who was a servant at the farm. Brotherton was the worse for drink and unfortunately made more noise than was desirable under such circumstances. The result was that Mr Atkinson and the other occupants of the farm, who had gone to bed, were soon awake. Suspecting it to be a

gang of thieves about to enter the house, Mr Atkinson, in fear and anxiety, ordered one of his male servants to seize a gun and shoot. Brotherton received the shot full in the breast and ran off some distance into the fields, where his dead body was discovered the following morning. A verdict of excusable homicide was returned.

Eighteen

BARBAROUS MURDER

Weeton, 1847

What the *Harrogate Advertiser* called one of the most diabolical murders it had ever been their lot to record was committed at Weeton, in July 1847. Three-year-old Maria Breton was murdered by her father, Francis Breton. William Bright, a lodger in Breton's house, told how he was woken in the early hours by noises and moaning in the room below, which was occupied by Breton, his wife and child. He immediately went downstairs, and saw Breton hit Maria three times with a poker, which Breton held in both hands. Bright immediately seized Breton and handed him over to the constables. They found the poor child with her head awfully mangled and blood and brains scattered on the floor and walls of the cottage. It appeared that Breton had taken the opportunity of committing the dreadful act during the temporary absence of his wife.

At his trial at York Assizes the question for the jury was, 'was Breton of sound mind?' Mr Anderson, the surgeon at York Castle, said he had seen him several times since his committal to the castle and was of the opinion he was insane and would not understand the nature of a plea. This was confirmed by Mr Noble, the governor of the castle. Another witness said before the murder Breton had been committed to Clayton Asylum but had escaped and had wandered the country for some time. On Sunday he had returned home and the next day killed his child.

The judge then directed the indictment be read to Breton, after which he asked him if he had heard the charge read, and if he understood it. Breton answered yes to both questions. The judge then asked, 'What is the charge?' To which Breton replied he did not know. The judge then asked Breton if he had ever been told he was charged with the murder of his child. Breton replied that he did not know the child was dead, and he'd never seen it since.

The judge asked if he understood the charge against him, to which Breton replied that the lodger came down the stairs and took the poker out of his hand. Several other questions were put to Breton to which he gave equally incoherent answers. The judge then asked the jury if they thought Breton was in a state of mind that would allow him to be placed on trial. They immediately replied they were of the opinion Breton was insane. He was consequently ordered to be confined at Her Majesty's pleasure.

Nineteen

SUPPOSED MURDER OF A FATHER BY HIS TWO DAUGHTERS

Harrogate, 1848

The inhabitants of Harrogate were thrown into a state of unusual excitement on 15 July 1848, when a rumour went round the town that an old man named Joseph Stubbs had been murdered by his two daughters, Sarah and Abigail. A reporter from the *Harrogate Advertiser* went hotfoot to the scene and interviewed Mrs Ann Stubbs, wife of the deceased and mother of the two girls. Mrs Stubbs took in washing, and was assisted by her daughters. She said she had earned 3s 2d and had given each a shilling for their work but they were not satisfied with this and began abusing her in a most shameful manner. She told her husband, who was present, and who had taken her side, to throw the girls and their possessions out of the house. On hearing this, the girls went upstairs. Mr Stubbs followed but as he reached the top of the stairs he was thrown down and fell violently on his head. Mrs Stubbs at once rushed to her husband's side, but he was fatally injured and died a few minutes later. She added that he had always been kind to her and an ill word had scarcely passed between them.

The *Harrogate Advertiser* reported that the two girls each bore a bad character, their conduct towards their parents was known to have been disgraceful in the past, and those who knew them were not surprised at the dreadful act which, if not premeditated, displayed an amount of hardened feeling they (the *Harrogate Advertiser*) had seldom met with.

An inquest was held at the Commercial Inn, Harrogate, two days later on 17 July. It was set for 6.30 p.m. but, owing to an unexpected detention on the road, the coroner, John Wood of York, did not arrive until 7.20 p.m. Mrs Stubbs told the jury that Mr Stubbs was aged about sixty-three, a labourer and a keeper of donkey carriages. Before this he had been a farmer. He lived in Tower Street with his wife, their two unmarried daughters, Sarah aged twenty-six and Abigail aged twenty-three, and a little granddaughter, Eliza, aged six. He was a very steady man, but a lady had given him a shilling and he had drunk two or three glasses of ale that morning. Also he had had nothing to eat in his own house for two or three days because his mind had been much disturbed by the conduct of his daughters, who had recently been cohabiting with some navvies. At about half past eleven on the morning of Saturday 15 July Mrs Stubbs and her daughters had a disagreement. Her husband, who was shaving, rose up and said he would let them know who was master, and struck Sarah. He then left them and went upstairs saying he would fetch down their boxes. She (Mrs Stubbs) then went out and went down the street calling for a policeman, but her little grandchild called her back by saying, 'Grandfather has fallen down stairs.' She then went back into the house and found her daughters holding her husband's head. Abigail said he had fallen down the stairs. Mr Stubbs was unable to speak and died without saying anything. Abigail began to cry and said she wished she had died instead of her father.

Six-year-old Eliza Stubbs was called as a witness, and the coroner put a number of questions to her, but her evidence was deemed inadmissible because of her young age.

Elizabeth Wilson, who lived next door but one, said she had heard a strange quarrelling from the Stubbs's house. Mrs Stubbs had come out and said, 'They've killed the old man. Where's the police? Which of you will go for the police?' She (Elizabeth) continued to hear quarrelling in the house. No one dared go in to interfere, so she went in herself. When she got half way up the stairs she heard a great scuffle in the

Tower Street, Harrogate, one time home of the Stubbs family.

garret, and dared go no further. She called out, Abigail! But no one answered. She then called out, Sarah! But again no one answered. She heard Abigail say to her sister, 'Damn him, throw him downstairs.' Then, 'Kill him, an old devil.' Fearing they would throw the old man on top of her, she hurried downstairs and returned to her own house. A few minutes later some women told her the girls had killed their father.

Ann Stevenson, an unmarried woman who lived next door to Mr Stubbs, said she heard a great noise and went into the street. Through the open door she saw Mr Stubbs and Sarah fighting in the kitchen, and Mrs Stubbs and Abigail fighting in the sitting room, and heard some 'curious expressions' used. Mrs Stubbs broke away and went up the street saying she would fetch the police. Ann then heard a great scuffle and fighting in the garret, and heard one of the daughters say 'Damn him, kill him.' and one say, 'Throw him down stairs.' She then heard the crash of Mr Stubbs falling down the stairs.

Joseph Young, a police officer, said he was crossing the Stray when little Eliza stopped him and told him her aunts had killed her grandfather. He went immediately to the house and found Mrs Stubbs in the kitchen with her two daughters. Mrs Stubbs told the two girls they had killed their father. They made no reply but were crying. Young went upstairs and found Mr Stubbs laid on his back in an upstairs room, apparently dead. He sent for a doctor then cautioned the two girls to be careful what they said as their words might be used afterwards in evidence against them. Sarah and Abigail said their father had gone upstairs to throw down their trunks and they had followed him. In the scuffle that followed he had held Sarah on the bed and struck her in the face several times. Abigail had seized him and pulled him off. He had tried to strike Abigail but his foot had slipped and he fell down the stairs. Young told them it was his duty to take them into custody for causing the death. He then took both girls to the Harrogate lock-up.

Mr Parry, a surgeon, told the inquest Mr Stubbs was dead when he arrived. He had carried out a post-mortem examination on the body and had found no external marks of violence sufficient to have caused death. He found Mr Stubbs had not eaten for some days, and it was his opinion that this, the struggle with his daughters, who were two strong women, and the fall down stairs had caused him to faint and death had ensued. He added that Mr Stubbs had fallen down stairs heels first.

In summing up, the coroner told the jury that if it appeared to them the old man had been thrown down the stairs by his daughters a verdict of manslaughter must be given. A verdict of murder could not be returned because there must be evidence to prove malice aforethought and premeditation. An open verdict could be given if there appeared to be no evidence to show who had thrown the deceased down the stairs, or even that he was thrown down the stairs. This would leave the police officer in a position to obtain further evidence and institute before a bench of magistrates any further inquiry that might be thought necessary.

At 10.20 p.m. the jury delivered their verdict. They found Mr Stubbs had died of exhaustion and fainting occasioned by his falling down stairs, but whether he accidentally fell down or was thrown down there was no satisfactory evidence.

This verdict disappointed the *Harrogate Advertiser*, who said their faith in law and humanity had been shaken by the decision of the jurors as unwarranted by the evidence of the witnesses, whose word proved a clear case of manslaughter if ever such a charge were proved.

On 19 July the case was heard before the magistrates. Hannah Murgatroyd, who lived at Apperley Bridge, near Bradford, and had come to Harrogate to see her father, who lived in Tower Street, said she had seen Mr and Mrs Stubbs struggling with their two daughters, and Abigail, after going up stairs, had shouted to her father, 'If you come up here I'll throw you down and break your neck.'

Sarah Stubbs said there was a quarrel between her, her sister and her mother. Her father came in and struck her. Her mother told him to throw their boxes downstairs. She sat down crying. On hearing the sound of a box, or something heavy, she went to the first floor landing where she found her large wood box. She took it upstairs and put in on an empty bed in the garret and found her father pulling other boxes into the room. She said, 'Oh father, what are you doing?' and he struck her again. Abigail came in answer to her screams and said, 'Oh father what are you going to do with her?' He then tried to strike Abigail. Sarah then went downstairs and did not see her father again until he had fallen down the stairs, when she immediately got some cold water and ran to help him.

Abigail said that, on hearing her sister scream, she ran upstairs and said to her father, 'Do be quiet and leave her alone.' She took Sarah her by the hand and pulled her away and she (Sarah) went downstairs to the back bedroom. Her father attempted to strike her but slipped and fell from the top of the garret stairs to the bottom. She got hold of him as soon as she could and called Sarah to fetch him a drink of water. A Mrs Watson and a Mrs Saville also came to help. She said neither she nor her sister spoke any angry words to their father. He had always behaved well to them in every respect and consequently they should be very sorry for any injury to him whatsoever. There was no one else in the house, and the doors and windows were all shut. Some of the evidence given against her and her sister, she said, had been given through malice.

The two girls appeared at York Assizes on 26 July 1848 where the jury wasted no time in finding them not guilty and they were set at liberty.

The case caused a sensation in Harrogate. Luckily for the *Harrogate Advertiser* it occurred in the summer (the paper was not published in the winter months) and such was the demand for news that the paper produced an extraordinary edition. However, the downside was it occurred when the town was full of visitors on whom the town's prosperity depended and who might be driven away by such goings on, but the *Advertiser* reassured them with the statement, 'We regret that Harrogate should have been the scene of such a melancholy piece of business and trust that stranger visitors will not take it is a thing of common occurrence amongst us.'

Twenty

ATTEMPTED MURDER OF
A BRIDEGROOM

Bishop Thornton, 1849

George Pullan and his bride were married at Bishop Thornton, a village about six miles north-west of Harrogate, on 8 September 1849. Unfortunately, the bride's father, Richard Scott, a forty-seven-year-old brick maker, objected to the wedding. That evening, as the happy couple were celebrating at the house of the bridegroom's grandfather, Scott appeared with a loaded gun, which he held to the breast of Pullan and pulled the trigger. Miraculously the gun failed to go off, although it was later found to be loaded with powder and shot, and there was a percussion cap on the nipple.

Having failed to shoot him, Scott then struck Pullan with the barrel of the gun, cutting his head, but before he could inflict any more injury Scott was seized by the wedding guests, disarmed and thrown out of the house. Undaunted, he later managed to force his way back in through a window and get into the bedroom, where he demanded his daughter return the clothes she had. He then followed the bride and groom into the road and threw stones at Pullan, all the time swearing and cursing at him. He had, somehow, managed to regain possession of the gun, and threatened to shoot Pullan. He pulled the trigger more than once, again with no result. Eventually John Turner, a constable, arrived and took the gun from him. He drew from it the shot and then fired the remainder of its contents into the air.

Scott was Pullan's employer, but why he objected to the marriage was not stated; it was assumed he considered Pullan beneath his daughter, although Pullan was said to be honest and industrious. At his trial the jury found Scott guilty of attempting to discharge a gun with the intention of doing some grievous bodily harm, but they strongly recommend him to mercy owing to the great state of excitement he was labouring under. He was sentenced to six months imprisonment with hard labour.

Twenty-One

SACRILEGE AND ROBBERY

Kirkby Malzeard, 1850

A sentence out of all proportion to the crime committed was passed on two men in 1850. Following a baptism at Kirkby Malzeard on 30 January that year, the church was safely locked up. The following day, the curate heard that Grewelthorpe church, just over a mile away, had been broken into. He therefore went to the Kirkby Malzeard church to check all was safe, but found it too had been broken into. Inside he found the iron safe had been taken from its place. Fortunately the communion plate had been removed for safe keeping and all the thieves managed to get away with was eight bottles of wine. A few days later two men, John Wilson (twenty) and Charles Lancaster (twenty-three) were arrested in York. They had left their lodgings in Ripon saying they were going to Darlington. They had been seen in the Kirkby Malzeard area and their boots matched boot prints found in the church. Lancaster said there had been a third man, but he was not caught. Both men appear to have had criminal records for they were sentenced to be transported for twenty years.

The church at Kirkby Malzeard.

Twenty-Two

MULTIPLE STABBINGS

Otley, 1850

What the *Leeds Intelligencer* called 'one of the most diabolical outrages ever perpetrated by Englishmen in civilised society' was perpetrated at Otley in the early hours of Sunday, 21 April 1850. Four navvies, employed in making a reservoir for supplying a woollen cloth manufactory with water at Burley Wood Head, had spent most of the previous day drinking in the Red Lion in Kirkgate, Otley. They were, George Tollerton (thirty-two), Robert Farrar (thirty-eight), Nathaniel Scholey (twenty-six), all originally from Wakefield, and William Jaques (twenty-nine), originally from Gainsborough. Jaques had come to the Otley area to work on the construction of the Leeds & Thirsk Railway and was known as The Gunner, or the One Eyed Gunner.

They had left the Red Lion at midnight, quietly, but the worse for drink. On leaving, one stole a live fowl belonging to the landlord, Henry Roundell. They walked up Westgate, which led to Burley Wood Head, where they lodged. In doing so they began to smash windows. Some with stones, others with their fists, at the same time uttering threats to the occupiers of the houses whose windows they smashed. The noise attracted Henry Thornes, a clerk in the Post Office, who lived in Westgate. He went out in his slippers and, together with John Oliver, a woolcomber, followed the men. When they got to the Fleece Inn they split up. Thornes followed the men to Piper Lane, at the top of Westgate. On his way he met William Ives, an Otley shoemaker, who was on his way home from Guiseley. Here they were rejoined by Oliver. Thornes asked the navvies, calmly, to pay for the windows they had broken. In reply one put his fist in Thornes' face and said he would pay him with that.

Ives had been jostled by the men prior to his meeting Thornes and one of the navvies, Tollerton, now asked him if he wanted to fight, and struck him in the mouth with his hand, causing Ives' mouth to bleed a little. Ives retaliated by striking Tollerton over the head with his walking stick with such force that Tollerton was knocked down. Thorne, Ives and Oliver then ran away, chased by three of the navvies, who threatened them with violence, but gave up the chase after about 100 yards.

Elizabeth Dawson, after hearing some noise in the street, went to her door to throw some water out and saw two of her neighbours, Sarah Kershaw and Mary Dickinson, standing outside. One of the women asked Tollerton if he had been hurt, to which he

The Red Lion, Otley, where the four navvies spent the day drinking.

replied, 'Yes they have nearly cut my head in two.' He wiped his hand down his head as if wiping blood off. Mrs Dawson said later she saw no blood, but Sarah Kershaw said Tollerton's head was badly cut. Mrs Dawson then saw one of the other navvies coming up the street, swearing and breaking windows with his fists. Her husband, Robert Dawson, who had also come out, put his hand on the man's shoulder and asked him if he knew what he was doing, but instead of answering him the navvy dragged him into the street and, with two others, began to punch him. Mrs Dawson at once ran to the Fleece, for assistance, screaming, 'They are killing my Bob, they are killing my Bob.' Mary Dickinson went to Dawson's assistance and grabbed one of the navvies, who told her to let go or he would kill them both. She replied, 'Don't kill this poor man, for he's a wife and seven children and we're both innocent.' The threat was repeated and she was stabbed in the hip.

At the Fleece Mrs Dawson asked William Oldfield, a mechanic of Burley, and Jonas Rhodes, a cloth dresser, who had heard her screams, to fetch a constable as some men were killing her husband. Oldfield did not know where the constable lived, but he and Rhodes went with her. On their way Rhodes was grabbed by a navvy and held, whilst a second asked what party he was for. They then let him go and one went and kicked in a window.

In the meantime, Robert Dawson's brother, John, who lived in Piper Lane, had come to his brother's assistance. When Mrs Dawson, Rhodes and Oldfield reached the Dawsons' house they found John Dawson lying dead on his own doorstep, having

The Fleece, Otley, where Mrs Dawson asked for help.

been stabbed in the thigh. Whilst Oldfield was looking at the body, Jaques took him by the collar and drew something across his throat and said, 'D**n thee, thou little ——, I am man enough for thee, although I have but one eye.' He then went away. Oldfield did not see what Jacques had in his hand, but on examining his collar and neckerchief found them to have been cut.

Sarah Kershaw, with the help of a woolcomber called Charles Pulleyn, had managed to rescue Robert Dawson from the navvies and take him inside. He was bleeding profusely from a deep knife wound in his cheek. Once inside one of the navvies tried unsuccessfully to break down the door and threatened to kill them all.

The noise in the street had disturbed George Swales, a tanner, who lived at 13 New Club Houses. He went out and asked one of the navvies what was up. The navvy put his hand on Swales's arm and left a bloody mark, but did not hurt him. Two of Mrs Kershaw's young daughters were stabbed, but fortunately none of the wounds were severe. Three of the navvies then ran about with knives in their hands, threatening to stab everyone they came near. David Ferrand, who lived next door to John Dawson, and who had been awoken by Mrs Dawson screaming, shouted to the navvies from a window, 'You have murdered that man.' At this the navvies began throwing stones at the window, and called out, 'They would kill all the —— in Otley.'

Constable William Brumfitt, alarmed at the disturbance, had dressed himself and reached the bottom of his garden just as the navvies were passing. He touched Farrar

Piper Lane, Otley.

and asked him what in the world they were about. The other three immediately rushed him and said, 'If this be the constable —— we can do for him.' They then dragged him to the middle of the road, tore open his waistcoat and tried to stab him in the breast. They also tried to cut a woollen scarf he was wearing around his neck so they could cut his throat. Fortunately he managed to free himself and the four men made off towards the Bradford toll bar swearing that 'they would make the earth open and stab all they met.' Brumfitt was later treated for a wound in his neck that needed stitches.

In the meantime Charles Pulleyn had gone to the White Horse Inn and enlisted the help of five men, who set off in pursuit of the navvies. These included James Thackeray, a currier, William Barret, a wool sorter, and Joshua Robinson, a butcher, who had armed himself with a poker. They caught up with three of the navvies on the Bradford road. Barret was cut behind the ear by Farrar. He (Farrar) and Tollerton were then knocked down by Robinson using the poker. Scholey was also knocked down, by Thackeray, and was later found to have a large bloodstained knife in his inside pocket. Jaques was apprehended at Burley later that morning.

At York Assizes in July all four pleaded not guilty to the charge of the wilful murder of John Dawson, a twenty-eight-year-old unmarried sawyer. It was not known which of the four had stabbed Dawson but the prosecution claimed all were guilty because they had acted with a common purpose. The defence argued the accused had been in good humour when in the Red Lion and had been provoked by Ives striking Tollerton a heavy blow on the head. This had been the cause of the disturbance. The stabbing of Dawson had been done in the heat of the moment. If the accused were guilty, they were guilty of manslaughter, not wilful murder. The jury agreed and found all four guilty of manslaughter. Tollerton, who it was considered had been provoked by Ives striking him, was sentenced to fifteen years transportation, the other three, transportation for life.

Twenty-Three

THE DISCOVERY OF A BODY ON ROCKING MOOR

Between Harrogate and Skipton, 1850

Rocking Moor is an expanse of moorland situated north of the more well-know Blubberhouses Moor, between Harrogate and Skipton. In May 1850 some men digging for turf on this moor near the village of West End discovered a body buried about 3ft below the surface. Both the Skipton and the Otley correspondents of the *Leeds Intelligencer* sent in reports, which contradicted each other in some details. The editor of the *Intelligencer*, not knowing which version was correct, obviously thought it best to print both, together with an extract from the *Bradford Observer*.

The Skipton correspondent reported that the body was that of a man about twenty-six years of age, and because it had been buried in peat was in an almost perfect state of preservation, although the peat had tanned the flesh. The body was naked and had been covered with a leather apron. Part of a cloth waistcoat, and a pair of woollen stockings, without feet, were laid beside the body and it was assumed they had belonged to the dead man. From the age of the man, his height and hair it was supposed the body was that of Stephen Carling, who had mysteriously disappeared from Burnsall, about for miles away, eleven years earlier.

The Otley correspondent reported that the body was clothed, was in a state of decay and covered with ling, which had been cut from the moor for that purpose. He too reported the remains were believed to be those of Stephen Carling, a cattle dealer who had disappeared eleven years earlier. He claimed several people had identified the body from the clothes, and little things found in the pockets.

The *Bradford Observer* stated, at the time Carling disappeared a minute and extensive search had been made, but no trace of him had been found, and it was believed he had been murdered. He had been a very respectable person and of an excellent character. He had been in partnership with his cousin, Jonathan Bland, and it was said the last time he had been seen was with Bland near Pateley Bridge. Bland had been questioned at the time and had accounted for Carling's disappearance by saying he had absconded to America with a large sum of money. Bland claimed he had received several letters from Carling since. This explanation was thought unlikely as Carling had left behind all his best clothes, as well as 10 sovereigns. Bland had, on many occasions, been charged with having a guilty knowledge of Carling's disappearance, but nothing could be proved. It was, however, noted that Bland had grown remarkably timid over the years and was afraid to go home alone at night. The body unearthed was in a remarkable state of preservation because of the peat, and had been immediately identified as that of Carling. His clothes were also well preserved and were instantly recognised by the tailor who had made them. In the pockets a comb and a handkerchief were found. These had been owned by Carling's then girlfriend, who had since married. The stockings (which had very unusual tops) were identified by the woman from whom Carling had purchased them. The reported ended with the statement that Bland had recently been apprehended at Skipton.

The following week, on 8 June 1850, the *Leeds Intelligencer* stated that in publishing the reports of their two correspondents, and the extract from the *Bradford Observer*, they may have done Jonathan Bland an injustice. This was because they had received an angry letter from Bland's father, Robert Bland, saying the reports were false and libellous, and unless his letter was published he would take legal action. According to Robert Bland, his son Jonathan and Carling had been in partnership as cattle dealers. At the end of December 1839 they had gone to York and Stamford Bridge fairs with a large drove of cattle, some of which they had sold. Carling had been left to sell the remainder and collect all the money. Carling was to have met Robert Bland at Skipton and hand over some money, but he never turned up. Jonathan then went to Lancaster and Preston fairs for ten days, and whilst there Carling absconded, leaving Robert to settle an account with the Craven Bank for which he was responsible. Fortunately the bankers had acted like gentlemen. Had they not done so Robert and his family would have found themselves in a serious situation.

Carling had gone to Appletreewick, where he called on William Inman and asked for the address of Inman's sister Mary, who had married a Phillip Joy and emigrated to America. Carling said he wanted the address because he was thinking of emigrating to America himself. The following year, 1840, Inman received a letter from Phillip Joy saying Carling had arrived in America safe and sound, and in good health, and was

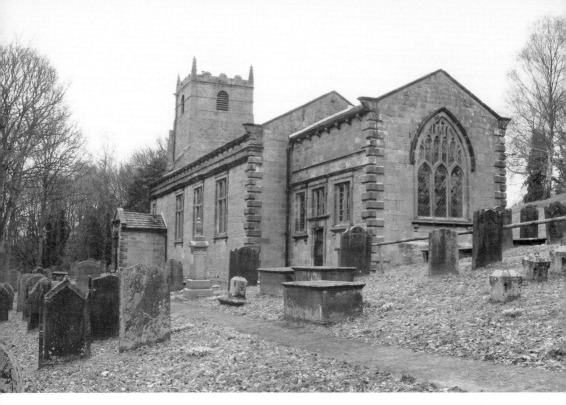

Fewston churchyard, where the body of the unknown man found on Rocking Moor was buried.

staying at his house. A short time later, a Halifax man, William Pickersgill, received a letter from Mary Joy of Richmond, America, (presumably Richmond, Virginia) saying Carling was working at a corn mill and earning £50 a year clear of all expenses. He had joined the Teetotal Society and was well liked by his employers. In another letter to Pickersgill, in 1843, Mary said Carling had left and she had not heard from him, although he had promised to keep in touch.

In June 1843 Mr Houghton of Tadcaster, a cattle dealer, received a letter from a Mr Anderson, a friend who had emigrated to America and lived in Fredericksburg. Anderson said he had met someone who knew him (Houghton). This was Carling, who had told Anderson he had left England in 1840.

Robert concluded by saying the people to whom the letters were sent still had them and the letters might be seen on request. He also said the rumours which were circulated at the time of Carling's disappearance were started by a woman who called herself an 'old witch' who happened to be in the neighbourhood at the time.

The body unearthed was taken to the Gate Inn, West End, where an inquest was held. Despite its apparent well-preserved state, its identity remained a mystery. There were no marks of violence on the body, and a post-mortem failed to find any clue as to the cause of death. The jury consequently returned an open verdict and the unknown man was buried in Fewston churchyard.

Twenty-Four

ATTEMPTED MURDER

Kearby with Netherby, near Harewood, 1852

Francis Long, was a twenty-four-year-old cattle dealer, who lodged with Grace Atkinson, aged thirty-seven, and her husband, a carpenter, at a house situated some distance from a public road at Kearby with Netherby, near Harewood. Also living in the house were a Mr and Mrs Appleyard. In October 1851, in consequence of Grace's bad language and rough behaviour towards him, Long decided to leave the house and obtain lodgings elsewhere. When he told Grace of this she flew into a towering passion, grabbed a gun, pointed it at him and threatened to shoot him if he did not change his mind. In view of this he consented to stay, but Grace continued her ill treatment of him as before. The result was that on 17 November he again told Grace he was leaving and gave her £45, which he owed for his lodging. Grace immediately grabbed a carving knife and threatened to stab him there and then if he didn't agree to stay. She then locked the doors of the house and put the key in her pocket. As a result Long stayed, but only until 8 December, when he succeeded in leaving, and went to lodge with a person named Mason.

Two days later Grace went to Mr and Mrs Appleyard and offered them a sovereign if they would go before the justices at Knaresborough and swear they had witnessed a criminal intercourse between her and Long in the kitchen of her home. The Appleyards refused to do so as they had witnessed no such thing.

On 29 January 1852 Grace went to a barn owned by Long, about a quarter of a mile from her house, and waited there a considerable time for Long to appear. Eventually Long brought some hay to the barn and was surprised to find Grace there. She begged him to go back to her house. She said her husband had recently purchased an estate in Kent and she offered Long a considerable sum to manage it as they, themselves, were not much acquainted with farming. Long refused and eventually Grace went away.

Some time previously Long had asked a man named Morrell to go to Grace's house and ask for a pair of scissors he had forgotten to take with him when he had left the previous December. Grace had refused to hand them to Morrell and had told him Long had to come for them himself. On the evening of the 29 January Long consequently went for the scissors and found Grace alone in the house. As he entered she locked the doors and kept the key. Long asked for his scissors. Grace mentioned the estate in Kent again, but Long said he thought she was making it up. He then asked her to repay £5 which he had overpaid for his lodgings. She replied the amount was upstairs and if he went upstairs with her she would pay him. When he replied there was no reason for him to go upstairs she pushed him towards the stairs and he went up. He led the way and as soon as he entered the bedroom Grace locked the door behind him, and from the outside said, 'There I've got you safe now.' At this Long went to the window and threw up the sash, only to see Grace standing below with a gun in her hand. Nevertheless, he climbed out of the window, prompting Grace to shout, 'If you come out here tonight I'll shoot you dead.'

Long was now hanging from the windowsill and was unable to climb back in. Unable to hang on any longer he let go and fell 15ft to the ground. Grace walked up to him as he lay on the ground and from a distance of two yards fired the gun at him, hitting him in the thigh. Long cried out in pain and asked Grace to fetch some assistance. She ran to the house of a person named Hannan and exclaimed, 'Oh dear, Long is shot.' Hannan returned with her and found Long bleeding profusely and in an exhausted state. A surgeon was sent for, who was obliged to amputate Long's leg, the injury being so great.

Grace appeared in court in March 1852 charged with having, on 29 January 1852, at Kearby with Netherby, discharged a loaded gun at and against Francis Long with intent to murder him. Long remained in a weak state and gave his testimony with some difficulty. Mr Bliss, defending, said the gun had gone off accidentally, such accidents happened even in the most experienced hands. He claimed Long had been thrown out of Grace's house and had returned to extort money from her. In her alarm she had locked him in the room and threatened to shoot him if he got out of the window. Being terrified and confused, the gun had accidentally gone off. She had run off in great distress for assistance, which tended to show she had shot Long by accident. The jury did not agree and found her guilty of shooting with intent to do some grievous bodily harm. She was sentenced to be transported for fifteen years.

Twenty-Five

A MOTHER EXHUMED

Knaresborough, 1853

When Hannah Bramley died, aged eighty-three, she was buried in the churchyard at Knaresborough. Two weeks after the burial a rumour swept Knaresborough that the real cause of her death had been the ill treatment she had received at the hands of her own daughter, a woman of dissolute habits. To satisfy the townspeople the body was exhumed and an inquest held at the Elephant & Castle Inn. Mr Beaumont, surgeon, made a post-mortem examination and stated that, in his opinion, the old woman had died from the effects of inflammation of the lungs, brought on by cold, and not from the effects of ill-treatment. Consequently the jury returned a verdict to that effect and the body was reinterred.

Twenty-Six

A WOMAN SCORNED

Knaresborough, 1855

Jean Lund, aged thirty-four, lived in Knaresborough with Edwin Harrison, a millwright. They were not married but had three children. In 1854 Harrison left her and went to live in Hull, where he married someone else. On 23 August 1855 news reached Jean that Harrison and his wife were in the Dog and Pheasant public house in Knaresborough. She went there at once, carrying a jug containing a pint of oil of vitriol (sulphuric acid). On seeing Harrison and his wife she said to Harrison, 'You are the devil I want,' and threw the oil of vitriol at them. Harrison's clothes were burnt, but he escaped injury. His wife, however, was severely burnt on the face and arm by the fluid. The landlady of the pub, Mrs Ware, was also very much burnt. When taken into custody Jean expressed no regret and said, 'I wish I had burnt Harrison's heart out'.

In throwing the vitriol she had spilt some on her hands and dress and had severely burnt them. At her trail the jury found her guilty, but recommended mercy. She was sent to prison for a year.

Twenty-Seven

ASSAULT

Between Farnham and Burton Leonard, 1857

Before the age of motor transport people in rural areas had often little option other than to walk between villages, and occasionally they met undesirables on the road. In June 1857 Elizabeth Buck was walking from Knaresborough to Bishop Monkton, a distance of about 6 miles, when she met two men at Walkingham Warren, about midway between Farnham and Burton Leonard. They asked how far it was to Ripon. After Mrs Buck gave an answer one of the men followed her, grabbed her around the neck, threw her down and held her there while the other man struck her hands several times with a stick. He then struck her face and body with his fists. The other man continued to hold her by the neck and blood began to flow from her nose and mouth. One of the men pulled off her pocket, but threw it away when he found it contained no money. He then ran away. The other man still had hold of Mrs Buck and wanted to drag her into some bushes, and threatened to murder her unless she went. Fortunately, at this moment Isaac Welham, gamekeeper to James Brown of Copgrove, came along. On seeing him, the man attempting to drag Mrs Buck into the bushes fled and hid in a hedge bottom, but Welham managed to capture him. He was Thomas Tasker, aged eighteen, and at his trial was sentenced to two years imprisonment with hard labour. The other man was not caught.

Twenty-Eight

MURDERED BY HER LOVER

Darley, 1858

In 1858 Stump's Lane was a narrow byroad running from the village of Darley to the Harrogate and Skipton turnpike road. It rose rapidly for the first quarter of a mile and was bounded on each side by a low stone wall. The road itself was rough and uncomfortable to travel over, both for pedestrians and horses. At the bottom of the lane, at Darley, was a row of cottages and at the top of the hill two farmhouses. Other farmsteads lay to the right and left, at a distance of a few hundred yards.

At about half past nine on the evening of Sunday, 1 August 1858 a schoolmaster's wife at Fringill, near Darley, heard dreadful screams. They were also heard by her daughter, who was walking from Fringill to Darley. So awful were they the daughter immediately turned around and returned home.

At 5 o'clock the following morning Richard Howard, known as Potter Dick, a Darley glass and china dealer, left home to collect a horse he had pastured nearby. He had gone about 300 or 400 yards when, in the ditch bottom in Stump's Lane, he discovered the dead body of a female, who he later recognised as Mary Jane Scaife, the twenty-one-year-old daughter of Thomas Scaife, a respectable farmer, who lived in Fringill. Her head was nearly severed from her body and her dress torn and covered with clotted blood, as were her face and the right side of her neck. She was laid with her head up the hill, her knees doubled under her and her feet inverted. Her face was fearfully distorted, with her mouth and eyes open. All her things were thrown about. These included a bonnet, a sort of headdress made of velvet, also a bow of ribbon, a prayer book and a parasol, saturated with blood, the handle of which was broken off, and laid near it. The ground where the body lay had been much disturbed over a small area. She and her murderer had evidently lain on the bank side.

Once he had recovered from the shock, Howard went home and told his neighbours there had been a murder. He then returned to the body with his wife and a neighbour, John Woodhead. In the next few minutes several other neighbours also came, including Mr Horton, the surgeon. Woodhead then left to fetch PC Clifton. After the body had been examined by Horton, PC Clifton ordered it removed to the New Inn at Darley.

Here Horton made a further examination and formed the opinion that some of the cuts had been made after the fatal one.

Mary Jane had been in the habit of sometimes staying the night with her uncle, Mr Downes, a tanner. She was therefore not missed at home that night. The main suspect was James Atkinson, Mary Jane's boyfriend. The two had been sweethearts since childhood and had wanted to marry. Unfortunately her mother, and his father, disapproved. Mary Jane had been sent away to Manchester to act as a nursemaid in a gentleman's service, but after twelve or eighteen months she had returned home in 1857. She had then broken off her relationship with Atkinson and begun to see a young man named Jeffery Gill. This affair, however, did not last long and after a few months she renewed her relationship with Atkinson. In March 1858 Mr Horton had, at Atkinson's request, treated Mary Jane for a miscarriage. On 27 July 1858 Atkinson went to Bewerley Gala and saw Mary Jane talking to Gill and was said to have been greatly annoyed.

On Sunday afternoon, 1 August 1858, the day of the murder, Mary Jane went to Darley church, and in the evening to Hartwith church, about two miles from her home. On her return she met Atkinson. They walked together quite amicably. On reaching

Nidd Lane, Darley, where Atkinson and Mary Jane passed a group of men.

Darley, at about half past nine in the evening, they passed a group of men in Nidd Lane, one of whom, William Pullan, referring to the couple, said, 'You see these are old acquaintances, they stick very close to each other.' Atkinson replied, 'Not so close as some of you think on.'

Atkinson's father was Thomas Atkinson, a flax spinner and a gentleman of some local position, who possessed considerable property. On going to Thomas Atkinson's home, PC Clifton found James Atkinson in the bedroom and charged him with feloniously cutting Mary Jane's throat. Atkinson replied, 'I have murdered my sweetheart.' Clifton took him into custody, and then took him to the New Inn, at Darley to check the body had been taken there as he had instructed. At the New Inn Atkinson asked to see the body in order to give her one last farewell kiss. This request was denied by the surgeon, because the coroner had not yet seen the body. Then, after being asked where the knife was, Atkinson took Clifton across three fields to a hole in a dry stone wall, where he had hidden the knife the night before. It was an ordinary clasp knife with two blades. It was bloodstained and the big blade was open.

Atkinson seemed much agitated, but quite sensible. He was taken first to Pateley Bridge and then to Ripon. On the way to Ripon he said voluntarily, 'I have had it on my mind for three weeks previous, and have threatened her and gotten her by the throat and said I would murder her if she would not have me.'

At Ripon, on being charged with the murder of Mary Jane Scaife, he said, 'I have been very happy since I left Pateley Bridge. I have committed a great crime but I am

Stump's Lane Darley, looking towards Darley.

quite content. I go freely to the gallows. I can forgive the vilest of the vile. I am guilty. I left her about half past nine o'clock last night.'

He was then remanded until the following Wednesday. On leaving the dock he said, 'Gentlemen. I hope to meet you all in heaven.' The next day he was taken to Knaresborough, where he appeared before the magistrates.

Horton had known both Mary Jane and Atkinson. He said he had never treated Atkinson except for an occasion accident, such as a trapped finger. He had always considered him to be of weak mind, and of no steadfast determination. He could not say he was insane, but he had a most irritable temper.

Thomas Atkinson, the brother of James Atkinson, said between four and five on the Monday morning his brother had come into his room and told him he had committed murder. He said, 'I have cut Mary Jane's throat. Lord have mercy upon me.' Thomas told his parents, and soon after PC Clifton arrived and arrested James.

James Atkinson made a full confession. He said the reason he murdered Mary Jane was because she would not have him. She believed they could not be happy because her parents and his father were against them. She also believed if they were married he would treat her badly, and suggested they go without each other a little. He told her he could not be happy without her and he would murder her if she would not have him. They walked on to Stump's Lane bottom. When they got a little way up she took her arm out of his. He wanted her to put it in again but she would not. He thought there was someone else she wanted and could not bear anyone else to have her.

He then took hold of her. She was all the while very awkward with him and would not go quietly. He took her by the throat and told her he would murder her if she did not go quietly. Then he took her by the throat and tried to choke her. She cried out, and, thinking someone would hear, they got up and walked on a little. He then pulled his knife out and showed it to her. She cried out, 'Let's go home Jim, let's go home.' He seized her and cut her throat and she cried out, 'It's all my mother that's caused this disturbance. The Lord help me.'

He then went across a field to a little dam where he washed the blood off his hands and face, then went home, but could not rest and told his brother.

When he had finished his confession he appeared as if a great burden had been lifted from his mind, and signed his confession with as much coolness as if it had been an ordinary witness statement.

Atkinson appeared at Leeds Assizes on 16 December 1858 charged with the wilful murder of Mary Jane Scaife. When asked if he pleaded guilty or not guilty he did not answer. He was asked twice more but still did not answer. On the fourth time of asking, after a slight pause, he said in a low voice, 'What do you mean? What do you mean?' He was asked again whether he pleaded guilty or not guilty, but did not answer. William Anderson, surgeon at York jail, was consequently called and told the court he had had frequent conversations with Atkinson, and believed him to be quite capable of understanding ordinary language. The judge said he could enter a plea on behalf of the prisoner but first he was legally bound to ask the jury to consider whether Atkinson was intentionally mute, or mute by the visitation of God. After a few minutes' deliberation the jury returned a verdict that the prisoner was mute by malice. The judge then entered a plea of not guilty on Atkinson's behalf.

There was no doubt Atkinson had killed Mary Jane. The question for the jury was, was he insane or not at the time of the murder. The court was told at least six of his close relatives suffered from serious mental illness, including a younger brother who had died aged about eight. Schoolteachers told how his weak intellect and poor attendance had made teaching him difficult. He could read a little but could not do arithmetic, and knew nothing of the New Testament. He worked in his father's mill, oiling the machinery and seeing the threads were all of a proper size. His father did not think him capable of keeping any books, or being entrusted with transactions involving money. He did, however, trust him to see the men kept to their work when he was absent, and had named him in his will as an executor.

Various witnesses were called who testified that he had a violent temper and flew into a rage over the slightest of things, especially when thwarted. A number of medical men, who specialised in the study of lunatics, were called, including John Kitching, the superintendent of the Retreat, an asylum near York. One had asked Atkinson if he was aware he was confined for a serious offence. Atkinson had replied that, a parson had said so, and a parson had told him it had to go before a judge. When asked about God he said he had never seen him and appeared altogether ignorant of the character of God, or where he was. When asked about Hell he said it was fire, and it might be in Yorkshire. When asked whether the Queen was a man or a woman he said she might be a man. When asked about Brimham Rocks (a visitor attraction about two and a half miles from Darley) he said he had heard of it, but could give no account of it, nor could he give an account of other places of interest in the locality. In their opinion Atkinson was an imbecile, a person whose mental powers had never matured beyond those of a child of nine or ten years of age. His mind, they believed, was not strong enough to control his animal instincts and passions, which were those of an adult. They did not believe Atkinson was feigning insanity.

Three letters written to relatives by Atkinson whilst in York Castle were read to the court. In them he expressed his great contrition at the murder and asked the forgiveness of God. He quoted a passage from the New Testament. There was some debate about whether the letters could have been written by a man who was insane. A Wesleyan minister had visited Atkinson in prison twice a week and there was further debate as to whether he had helped write the letters. Unfortunately, the minister had not been asked to attend court to give evidence.

The trial lasted three days. Some long speeches were made, one lasting three hours, another two. At the end of the second day the judge complained the case had been most outrageously spun out, and he had never heard so much time wasted in his life. A reporter present noted during the whole proceedings Atkinson had rather turned his head from the judge and jury, and there was nothing remarkable about his appearance that would give an impression he was deficient in intellect.

The jury were out for three and a half hours. On their return the foreman gave a verdict of guilty. Some jurors immediately shouted, 'not guilty'. The foreman then corrected himself and said, 'We find the prisoner not guilty on the grounds of insanity.' The judge then ordered Atkinson to be detained during Her Majesty's pleasure. Mary Jane was buried at Hartwith. Her crumbing tombstone bears the words:

> The victim of the murders blade
> Beneath a gory corse was laid
> Her soul we trust to realms has flown
> Where theft and murder are unknown.

Atkinson was in the news again a year later, in July 1859, when it was reported he had been guilty of outrageous conduct towards officials and others at York Castle, where he was confined. He had been violent towards his fellow prisoners, and might have seriously injured one if an officer had not intervened.

A year later, in February 1860, PC Clifton himself appeared in court, charged with assaulting Joseph Rhodes of Darley. On the 27 January Rhodes had called at the New Inn, and whilst there Clifton came in and challenged him to fight several times. Rhodes left the inn with two or three friends and when they had got to a place

Mary Jane's grave in Hartwith churchyard.

known as the New Row, Clifton overtook them and attempted to throw Rhodes down, struck at Rhodes's heels and wanted to fight. Rhodes said Clifton was drunk at the time and nothing was said to provoke him. This was confirmed by two witnesses. However, Mrs Darnborough, the landlady of the New Inn, said she could not tell that the policeman was the worst for liquor, and Richard Metcalfe, another witness, considered him quite sober. The bench considered an assault had been clearly proved, but because of Clifton's previous good character (against whom they had not been a single report) the mitigated penalty of £2, and costs of £1 4s 6d, only was inflicted, with the alternative being fourteen days imprisonment.

Twenty-Nine

A RIPLEY MAN EXHUMED

Ripley, 1858

Walter Houseman, a seventy-one-year-old Ripley farmer, went to meet two of his children, whom he had sent to Shaw Mills for a couple of pigs. On the road he met three farm labourers from Shaw Mills, William Windsor, Michael Sanderson and Thomas Carey. These three took away a little dog which accompanied one of the children, and, when Houseman attempted to get it back, the men beat him up. Mr Taylor, a farmer from Clint, went to his assistance and was himself beaten up by the three men, who then made off. Houseman later told a blacksmith named Carrington, they had knocked him (Houseman) down, punched and kicked him and struck him with stones.

The attack happened on 15 November 1858. A few days later Houseman began to feel ill and died on 23 November. Mr Cooper the surgeon at Birstwith, decided Houseman had died of apoplexy and the unfortunate farmer was buried on 27 November. Houseman's friends and relations, however, were not happy. They believed he had died as a result of the attack by the three men. The coroner consequently ordered Houseman's body to be exhumed and an inquest was held at the Star Inn, Ripley. A post-mortem was carried out by Mr Cautley, surgeon of Killinghall. He found a large bruise on the deceased's left arm and slight ones on the legs, but no injury likely to cause death. In his opinion death had not been caused by apoplexy, but by heart disease and inflammation of the lungs. The jury consequently returned a verdict that death had arisen from these causes, and the body was reburied.

Thirty

HIGHWAY ROBBERY

Near Hampsthwaite, 1859

William Goodyear, a farmer who lived at Whitewall, near Felliscliffe, went to Knaresborough market on 19 January 1859. He left in the evening with a horse and cart and overtook a man walking on the road between Knaresborough and Starbeck. The man said he was going to Skipton and Goodyear offered him a lift. At about midnight they arrived at the Nelson Inn, Saltergate, near Hampsthwaite. Despite the lateness of the hour, they obtained something to drink and after about an hour proceeded on their journey. When they got to Greyston Hill they got out of the cart and walked up the hill. Suddenly the man seized Goodyear by the throat, threw him down, struck him several times on the face and robbed him of his purse, which only contained about four or five shillings in silver. He then ran away, leaving Goodyear lying on the road badly injured. When Goodyear recovered his senses he went to the house of his son-in-law, Joseph Wrathall, a shoemaker at Greyston Plain, and told him what had happened. Police Constable Lamb, stationed at Hampsthwaite, was informed, given a description of the man, and, acting on information received, arrested him at Skipton. He was James Foulds, a known thief with previous convictions for robbery from the person. He lived in Skipton, but was originally from Colne in Lancashire. He denied having been on the road and of ever having met Goodyear, but was identified by both Goodyear and Mr Frankland, the landlord of the Nelson Inn. At his trial he was sentenced to three years penal servitude.

Thirty-One

A NEW-BORN BABY KILLED

Ripley Castle, 1870

At about a quarter to three on Sunday, 12 June 1870 Matilda Kirkley, a scullery maid at Ripley Castle, between Harrogate and Ripon, saw Margaret Marshall, an under laundry maid, who was known as Mary, come down the stairs and go into the water closet. After being in there about a quarter of an hour she came out, went into the wash house, and returned to the water closet with a pail full of water and a floor cloth. She said she had been sick. After some time she came out and Matilda noticed some blood marks on the handle of the pail. She asked Mary what was the matter, and Mary replied, 'Nothing. You need not be afraid.'

Soon after, Matilda found Mary on the seat of the water closet trembling. She asked her again what the matter was, and Mary replied as before. Matilda then heard a feeble noise and asked Mary what it was. She replied it was her insides. Matilda noticed that the floor had been washed and, beginning to feel afraid, went upstairs and returned with Elizabeth Mook, the kitchen maid. Elizabeth noticed blood on Mary's hands and clothes and heard a baby crying. She asked Mary if she had had a baby. She said not. She was then asked if she had had a miscarriage, and answered, yes. Elizabeth then sent for Mrs Crosier, the housekeeper, who ordered Mary be taken upstairs. They then assisted Mary upstairs and put her to bed, leaving the second laundry maid with her.

The butler, on being informed, sent for Matthew Harrison, a mason, and instructed him to be break the water closet into pieces. Before he began, and throughout the time he was pulling the water closet to pieces, Harrison could hear a child crying. When he had pulled the water closet to pieces he fastened a lighted candle to a piece of string and lowered it down the drain. By this light he saw a baby laid on its right side with its head up the main drain. He managed to place the baby on a coal rake it and draw it up,

Ripley Castle.

taking care not to press it against the side walls of the water closet. He then handed it to Elizabeth Mook. Although it had been down the drain for almost an hour the baby was still alive. Elizabeth washed it, wrapped it in flannel and sat it by the kitchen fire for a short time. She then gave it to Mrs Harrison, the wife of the mason. She tied the umbilical cord and attended to it in a proper manner. She gave it something to eat, and it cried very strongly at times.

At about half past four Jane Stott, washerwoman at Ripley Castle, and wife of the shepherd, was sent for and the baby placed in her care.

It wasn't until a quarter to eight that R.S.Veale, a doctor and surgeon in practice at Hampsthwaite, arrived, having received a message to attend immediately at Ripley Castle. He found the baby to be a full gown, fully developed male child. On further examination he found it very exhausted from loss of blood and thought its cry was very feeble. It had severe abrasions of the skin on its left cheek, left arm, left thigh and legs, and on the left ankle there was a very severe jagged wound cutting all the tissues down to the bone, and leaving exposed the ankle joint. The umbilical cord had been rudely torn and tied with a piece of worsted. It had not been sufficiently tied to stop the haemorrhage. There was no blood oozing from the cord, but there was considerable oozing from the jagged wound in the ankle.

Dr Veale tied the cord, dressed the ankle wound and ordered Mrs Stott to dress the abrasions with lint and oil. Instead of dressing the child he ordered him to be wrapped in cotton wool and flannel, because of his weakness, and to have milk and sweetened water given to it from time to time. Gin and water had been given to him

The Star Inn, Ripley (now the Boars Head Hotel), where the post-mortem on Mary's baby was carried out.

prior to the doctor's arrival. He then left the child in the care of Jane Stott and went to see the mother.

Despite Dr Veale's and Jane Stott's care, the child died at half past ten that night. Three days later Dr Veale was called to the Star Inn, Ripley, where the body of the unfortunate child lay, to carry out a post-mortem. Two fractures of the skull were detected, and it was his opinion the cause of death was exhaustion from loss of blood, accelerated by the injuries received on its head and ankle.

On 23 June Mr Howard, inspector of police at Harrogate, apprehended Mary Marshall at Ripley Castle and charged her with giving birth to a male child in the water closet on Sunday 12 June, and by some means allowing it to fall into the sewer beneath, by which it received wounds which afterwards caused its death. She made no reply. The water closet was in fact no water closet because no water was supplied to it. The pan was hewn out of a great block of sandstone rock. The hole was oblong and the edges sharp and jagged. The baby could not have passed through the hole without assistance. Mary later appeared at Knaresborough Court House where she was committed to the Wakefield House of Correction for trial at the next Leeds Assizes, charged with wilfully causing the death of a new-born male infant by forcing it down a water closet. She rocked to and fro and sobbed bitterly. Two of the witnesses, her fellow servants, fainted during the hearing and had to be assisted from the court.

The case was heard at Leeds Crown Court in August 1870. In summing up, the judge, Mr Justice Brett, pointed out to the jury that they might find Mary guilty of manslaughter if they believed she thought the child was not alive when she forced it down the water closet. The jury took this view and found her guilty of manslaughter. His Lordship then told Mary that the jury had saved her life; if they had found her guilty of murder she would have suffered the death penalty. She had, he continued, for her own selfish safety, in order to hide that which comparatively would be a slight shame, caused the death of her own child. She was not yet twenty years old and for years she must be separated from everybody that she had known, from her friends and kindred, from everything that had been a pleasure to her.

Mary, who appeared to be greatly distressed throughout the trial, pleaded, 'Oh have mercy' but his Lordship said while he had feelings of pity he would not be doing his duty if he listened to them. He then sent her to prison for ten years, and she was removed from the court in a half-fainting condition.

Two similar cases came became before the court later that day. Jane Anne Rose, a twenty-one-year-old spinster, and Sarah Ann Saxton, a thirty-year-old married rug maker both pleaded guilty to the crime of concealment of birth. Rose at Bilton with Harrogate on 15 April 1870 and Saxton at Dewsbury on 29 May 1870. In both cases the child had been stillborn. His Lordship was of the opinion most cases of concealment of birth arose because the courts dealt too leniently with such cases, which they treated as a light offence. He thought concealment of birth was a mere cloak for the destruction of the children. He had passed lenient sentences on such cases himself, but felt the time was coming, and for the public good must come, when concealment was not treated as a light offence. He said the fathers of the children are originally to blame, but the father is not guilty of concealing the birth. The father has nothing to do with that. The mother probably considered the father a bad, careless and cruel man, but he has nothing to do with the crime, and the law could not reach him. He then said he would not punish either woman severely, but in any future case the punishment would be more severe. He then sentenced both women to six months imprisonment with hard labour.

Thirty-Two

A SISTER MURDERED

Near Kirklington, 1874

A murder where the motive remains something of a mystery occurred on the evening of 5 May 1874. At about 5.30 the following morning John Marshall, a railway platelayer, walking along the path from the Ripon highway to Thornborough, discovered the body of a young girl in a wheat field, known as the barnfield, belonging to W. Horner. She lay on the bank of a mill stream, and had evidently been dragged there from the road. Her throat had been cut, almost serving her head from her body. Her necktie was drawn tight over the cut, and her clothes were disordered, and were up a little above the knees. The lower part of her dress was smeared with blood. Near to the body was an umbrella. She was identified as Elizabeth Jackson, the sixteen-year-old daughter of John Jackson, a Carthorpe labourer.

PC Hudson was informed and the body moved to the Golden Lion Inn at Kirklington. Here it was examined by Dr Mickle, who found no other marks of violence on the body. In the girl's pockets were two letters, a photograph of a young woman, a shilling, a hymn and a pair of kid gloves. The letter was from Edwin Gatenby, her former boyfriend, stating he had found someone else. The photograph was of the other girl.

What appeared to be bloody fingerprints were found on a stile at the entrance to the barnfield. Later a short pipe, marked with blood, was found in a near-by mill race. The police made a thorough search for a knife, or something of the kind. Gutters and hedgerows for miles around, especially in the neighbourhood of Upsland, and on the farms of Mr Smith and Mr Smurthwaite were searched. The mill race, in which the pipe had been found, was dammed and the bed of the stream raked. Parts of an army razor case were eventually found several yards apart, some in a field, and others in a hedgerow.

The last person seen with the deceased was her brother, William Jackson. Jackson was thirteen years older than Elizabeth, and was said to be fond of her. He had often sent her small amounts of money when away. He had been a soldier for nine years with the 77th Foot Regiment and had served in India, but latterly had been attached to the Army Reserve. When at Portsmouth he had received a severe blow on the head when in a fight with some costermongers and had been hospitalised for five weeks. After this he became quarrelsome when he had a drop of beer, and had been known to take off his clothes and throw them in the fireplace. When asked why, he replied, 'Oh it's my head that feels bad, but it's alright now.' He had been the best shot in the company, but after receiving another head wound this was no longer the case.

For the previous three weeks he had lived in the family home at Carthorpe. He was not often drunk, but when he was he was troublesome. On the 4 May he had come home drunk, had thrown a stool violently onto floor, and, when his father said he would fetch a constable, Jackson had said if he did there would be blood. He seemed to be crazy, and his parents were so afraid they locked themselves in their bedroom.

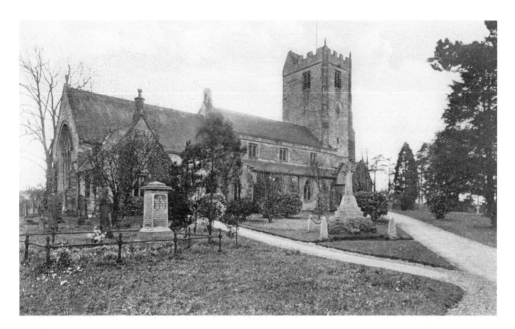

Kirklington church, where Jackson told his sister she had better go home.

Jackson senior told his son he could no longer tolerate his behaviour and he must leave. On the evening of 5 May Jackson set off for Ripon, about thirteen miles away, to look for work. Shortly before his departure his sister Elizabeth had set off for Kirklington, about one and a half miles away, to apply for a job. Jackson overtook her on the road and they went to James Husthwaite, a Kirklington shoemaker, leaving a slipper they wanted him to repair.

After leaving the shoemaker's shop Elizabeth said she would see him on his way to Ripon. When they got to Kirklington church he told her she had better go home as it was getting dark, but she said she would go a little further with him. They turned down the Ripon road, where they were met by Mr Wells, a farmer of Berry Hill, and one of his workmen. Jackson was smoking a pipe, and was a few yards ahead of Elizabeth. He repeatedly looked back at her, as if he wished her to hurry. Elizabeth seemed distressed, and there was something altogether peculiar about the appearance of both of them. Wells and his man watched them until they were out of sight, at a point within 100 yards of where she was subsequently murdered.

Elizabeth asked Jackson if she could go away with him but he refused. She said he would never write and started crying. Jackson walked away but she ran after him saying where he went she would go. Jackson then took out his razor and cut her throat. He then separated the handle, which was marked 77 14 LD, from the blade, and put the blade in a hedge on the left side of the road about a mile from Well on the Masham road. He then went to a farmhouse at Gybdykes near Masham where he spent the night in a barn.

The next day he started out for Bishop Auckland, to seek work with James Thompson, a timber merchant and farmer in the Ripon area. He stopped at a pawnbroker's in Darlington and pawned a coat and waistcoat for 11s, using the name Henry Gray. He then went to an inn at Walworth, where he told the inn keeper's wife, Mary Storey, that he had a sister to be buried the next day, and she had been murdered by her brother. When asked if he could give any account of it, he replied, 'No, they do not know what he did it for, without it was she would go with a young man that he was against her keeping company with.' (Jackson was said to have been against Elizabeth keeping company with Edwin Gatenby.) Mary Storey then said he must be a villain and must be hanged, to which Jackson replied, 'It's my opinion he went straight off to America and he will never be caught.' Mary Storey thought Jackson very troubled.

Jackson then managed to obtain a ride to West Auckland on a Mr Taplin's brewer's dray. He asked the drayman if he had seen the newspapers that day. When the drayman replied he hadn't, Jackson said, 'It will be in the papers today. My brother has killed my sister by cutting her throat.' The draymen told him not to talk so silly. Unfortunately for Jackson on leaving the dray he accidentally left behind his bundle, which contained shirts and socks with his name on. The police were informed and made a vigorous search in the pits, iron works and other places where he might have found work. On 9 May he was spotted by a man named Henry Booth in a back lane near West Auckland colliery. Booth immediately informed PC Wright, who, after a chase, arrested Jackson and charged him with murdering his sister. Jackson replied, 'Oh that's it is it?'

Jackson was taken to Northallerton Jail and then, on 18 May, to Wath police station. At Melmerby railway station, the station for Wath, a large crowd gathered, eager to see the prisoner, but were disappointed because he was brought, not by rail, but by road. At Wath police station, in a show of indifference, Jackson whistled whilst his handcuffs were removed. The whistling ceased when he was placed in a cell and on looking in it was discovered he had attempted to commit suicide by cutting his throat with a piece of tin he had sharpened and concealed for that purpose.

Because of his injury Jackson was unable to face the magistrates at Wath, but by August he was sufficiently recovered to be sent for trial at York Assizes. Whilst the trial was in progress James Edwards, one of the jurymen became so ill he was removed from the court, and a Leeds surgeon, Mr Scattergood, who was waiting to give evidence, was called to treat him. Mr Scattergood said Edwards would be unfit to continue that day but should be well enough by the morning. The trial was consequently adjourned, and Scattergood and the jury were locked in York Castle for the night.

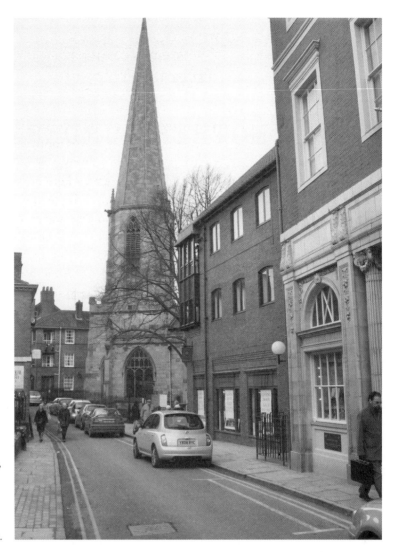

St Mary's, Castlegate, York, where the bells were tolled for fifteen minutes before and after the execution of Jackson.

The following day the trial resumed. It was considered that Jackson was not insane, and after being out for seven minutes the jury returned a verdict of guilty. The judge then passed sentence of death, but did not put on the black cap.

Although executions were no longer public, a large crowd gathered outside the castle gates in the hope of seeing Askern, the executioner, arrive. They were disappointed as he had arrived the night before and had stayed overnight in the castle. Jackson made a full confession, wrote out the 51st Psalm and sent it to his parents asking them to read it in remembrance of him. At 8 o'clock on the morning of 18 August the sentence of death was carried out. This was indicated to the crowd outside by a black flag being hoisted above Clifford's Tower. It remained there for an hour, the period it was customary for the body to be left hanging. The bells of St Mary's, Castlegate, were tolled for fifteen minutes before and fifteen minutes after the execution.

Thirty-Three

A MOTHER MURDERED
BY HER SON

Kirkby Malzeard, 1874

William Barker, a Kirby Malzeard farm labourer, was said to be a miser who had hoarded a considerable sum of money for a man in his position in life. The cottage in which he lived had been left to him by his father, who had also left him other property. He had three sons, John, Gordon and Alfred. John, aged twenty-three, had, at one time, been a butcher in Manchester but had done nothing for three months, having been ill with quinsy, although he thought it diphtheria. Gordon was a guard on the Leeds tramways. Alfred was thirteen years old.

In 1872 William's wife ran off with a man called Richard Wood, and took £100 of William's money with her. They were caught near Bridge House Gate, Pateley Bridge. Wood was sentenced to six months imprisonment, but Mrs Barker was acquitted. William appears to have forgiven his wife and afterwards treated her more considerately, but his son John, who had been called to give evidence against her, and appears to have inherited his father's miserly ways, was said to have watched her ever since to make sure she did not spend any penny which could be saved. There were frequent rows between mother and son. On one occasion, when she moved some of his clothes, he jumped out of bed and cut her head with the buckle of a leather strap, which he used as a garter, and chased her out of the house.

There were also rows between the brothers. On one occasion George had threatened to murder John, and their mother had to call in the local policeman. Their father had, himself, spent eight months in prison for threatening to kill a neighbour.

John's maternal grandmother, Ann Bonwell, had once been confined to a lunatic asylum for a few months and William began to doubt his son's sanity. John would sit in the house all day saying he was studying, but would not say what he was studying. Sometimes he lay in bed all day without eating. During the night he would check three or four times that the door of the house was locked, and would not have a candle lit, because he said people were watching the house. William had taken him to Ripon to work at peeling bark. He thought the company would do him good, but John had just looked at the men, and they could do nothing with him.

In desperation William went to the assistant overseer of the poor, Thomas Hudson, to ask if John could be admitted to an asylum. But Hudson was away from home, and continued to be away.

On 4 June 1874 William went to Ripon, seven miles away, with his son George. His youngest son, Alfred also went, but instead of going with his father went with a Mr Bland in his cart. William's wife was frightened of her son John and did not relish being in the house alone with him. She asked him to go to Ripon with his father and offered to treat him to a ride there, but he refused to go.

Between half past ten and eleven that morning Charles Frankland, a retired inn keeper and farmer, was in his mother's house, which was 10 to 15 yards from the Barkers' when he heard a noise. He said to his mother, 'There was a tremendous row next door,' to which his mother replied, 'Sit down and never mind.' He went outside, heard a rumbling noise in the cellar, and heard a kind of shriek, but could not tell if it was from a man or a woman. After standing a minute or two he went back inside and told his mother it was all silent now. She replied, 'It's nothing fresh, sit down.'

Alfred returned home on Mr Bland's cart and overtook his father on the road. William arrived home about a quarter to five in the afternoon and found Alfred lying on a sofa. John was also there, sitting in his usual chair. Surprised, his wife had not prepared a meal for them he asked John where she was. John got up and stood by his father, who was untying a little parcel. William again asked his son where his mother was. He replied, 'I have killed her.'

Thinking he was joking William said, 'Thou surely hasn't,' to which his son replied, 'I have father. I have chopped her head off with a bill,' or words to that effect. William did not believe him because, apart from the incident with the buckle garter, he had never known him strike his mother. He was very fond of her and often bought her presents. John then said his mother was in the cellar. Alfred was sent to take a look and in his absence William noticed blood on John's trousers, below the knee.

Alfred came up from the cellar in tears and said his mother was down there lying in a pool of blood. William then went down himself and saw his wife lying dead, with her head nearly cut off. She had been preparing to whitewash the cellar, and there was some whitewash partly mixed. A hedging bill lay on the shelf which looked like it had blood on it. On returning upstairs he told Alfred to go and fetch the policeman.

On the arrival of Police Constable Clarke, who was stationed at Kirby Malzeard, William pointed to John and said, 'He tells me he has killed his mother, take him away.'

John was taken to PC Clarke's house, which also contained the lock up. Here he was searched, but nothing but a handkerchief was found on him. It was noticed there were marks of blood on his clothing. PC Clarke then returned to the Barker's house and found William and Alfred in the cellar. The deceased was clutching a pair of spectacles, with one of her fingers through the place where the glass should have been. Beside her was a black straw hat, the inside of which was saturated with blood. There was a cut across the top and one of the strings was also cut.

In answer to the question 'What has he done it with?' William handed PC Clarke a bloodstained hedging bill from a shelf, and said, 'He must have done it with this bill.'

Mr Ledgard, the surgeon, was sent for and the body removed upstairs. To do this they had to pass out into the street. News of the murder had spread, and a large crowd had gathered. PC Clarke then returned to the lock up and charged his prisoner with wilfully killing Mrs Barker. He was then cautioned, and on being asked if he had anything to say, thought for about a minute and replied, 'No.'

He was then taken to the Ripon House of Correction, where he picked up a New Testament and read aloud the parable of the prodigal son to the two policemen who kept constant watch on him. An inquest was held at the Queens Head Inn, Kirkby Malzeard on 5 June, where a verdict of wilful murder was returned against him.

At his trial in August the jury found him not guilty of murder on the grounds of insanity and he was ordered to be detained in an asylum at Her Majesty's pleasure.

Thirty-Four

THROWING VITRIOL

Knaresborough, 1874

In November 1874 the thirteen-year-old son of Mr Herrington, a brewer of ginger beer, was charged with throwing vitriol in the face of the eleven-year-old son of Mr Barker, butler to Basil E. Woodd. Herrington's father had sent his son to fetch the vitriol, which was to be used in the manufacture of ginger beer. On his way home young Herrington stopped and played with Barker. When Barker asked what was in the jar Herrington said syrup, poured some into Barker's hands and threw some in his face. Fortunately none went into Barker's eyes, but his face and hands were blistered. In court the chairman reprimanded Herrington's father for sending such a young boy for such a dangerous article. He then ordered young Herrington to receive six strokes with a birch rod, and his father to pay the court and doctor's expenses.

Ripon House of Correction, now the Prison and Police Museum, where John Barker was taken after murdering his mother.

The Queen's Head Inn, Kirkby Malzeard, where a verdict of wilful murder was returned.

Thirty-Five

MANSLAUGHTER AT THE GENERAL TARLETON

Ferrensby, 1876

The General Tarleton public house at Ferrensby, near Knaresborough, is named after the British general, General Tarleton, who fought in the American War of Independence (1775-1783.) At about half past ten on the morning of 22 May 1876 four militiamen of the 5th West Yorkshire Militia, who were absent from the usual morning training of the regiment, went into the General Tarleton and asked Sarah Feasby, the live-in housekeeper, for a quart of beer. They drank the beer, but when asked for payment of 6*d* they objected to paying more than 4*d*. Robert Gibson, the landlord, said he could not afford to sell his beer for that money. The men were very awkward and called him bad names. As a result Gibson said he would not serve them any more beer. Just then, a woman came in with three children and asked if she might sing. She started singing but Gibson stopped her. One of the militiamen then got up and said he would sing, another danced, and all caused a great disturbance. Gibson told Mrs Feasby, in the presence of the men, he would go out and see if he could find George Barker, the blacksmith, or anybody else, to put them out. He then left. Whilst he was away Mrs Feasby asked the men to leave, and they did so. They were all rather the worse for liquor and went out dancing and singing. One carried a stick with which he hit a table on the way out, but they did not say anything about doing anything to the landlord, nor did they threaten Mrs Feasby.

Gibson was later described as a feeble man, which a little matter would knock down. On his speaking to George Barker, Barker asked Gibson why he did not turn them out himself. He replied he could not do it. In the blacksmith's shop was William Middleton, a postman, who had come to the end of his round and had called in to get a cart repaired. Gibson told Barker's wife he needed some assistance to turn some militiamen out of his house because they were kicking up a fine row. He said something about fighting, but Middleton could not tell what. Just then Peter Thompson, an Arkendale farmer, came down the road with three cows, and Gibson said, 'This is the man that will help me.' Gibson told Thompson a man wanted to fight him.

The General Tarleton, Ferrensby.

The militiamen then appeared. Gibson said to one of the militiamen, 'Now you may have a go.' He then turned to Thompson and said, 'Won't you fight him?' Thompson said he would not. The militiaman then said, 'I will fight either you, or him' and asked Thompson if he wanted to fight. Thompson replied, he had nothing to fight for and began to walk away. Suddenly, without any warning, the militiaman struck Gibson, who fell backwards, striking his head on the ground. Middleton turned to the militiaman and said, 'You've killed him.' At this the man turned pale, but Middleton did not hear him say anything. The other three militiamen did not interfere at all, or encourage the fourth to strike Gibson, but one said it served Gibson right. All four then walked off in the direction of Knaresborough.

Gibson remained flat on his back in the middle of the road, with Middleton and Thompson holding his head for about ten or fifteen minutes. Blood was coming from his mouth and he appeared to be insensible. Gibson's aunt, Mary Gibson, who lived near the blacksmith's shop, came out, sat him in a chair and wiped the blood from his mouth. He set his eyes fixed on her, but he did move his hands or speak. He was then carried into the General Tarleton. Sarah Feasby later said that when Gibson was assisted back to the General Tarleton by his nephew, Thomas Gibson, he did not appear very unwell and when she asked him shortly afterwards if he would have any dinner, he replied 'No.'

It was not until a little after ten in the evening that William Renton, a Knaresborough surgeon, arrived. He found Gibson in a state of almost complete coma, and evidently suffering from compression of the brain. He considered it a hopeless case. Next morning at a quarter past four Gibson died. He was fifty-six years old.

The soldiers of the West Yorkshire Militia were part-time soldiers, the Victorian equivalent of the Territorials. The next day, Middleton and a police sergeant, Ambrose Varley, went to Captain Story's house at the Knaresborough barracks. They were taken to the cells which contained a number of soldiers. A sergeant brought out the men and Middleton picked out the man who had struck Gibson. The sergeant then asked the man his name and company, to which he replied, James Bartley, Company D. Bartley looked very pale and asked Middleton what was the matter. Middleton said he was sorry for him but the man he had struck at Ferrensby was dead. Bartley made no reply. The police sergeant then handcuffed him and took him away. The three other militiamen, Thomas Ryan, Henry Ridge, and Fordy (Fordy's Christian name was not reported), were put under arrest in the militia guard room. Ridge was a Knaresborough man. Bartley was twenty-seven years old and a labourer. He lived in Silk Street, Manningham, Bradford, and had previous convictions, including one for burglary.

At an inquest at the Blue Bell Inn, Arkendale, the coroner told the jury if the four militiamen had, on coming out of the General Tarleton, combined together for the purpose of assaulting the deceased they would be equally guilty of any assault which was committed, but there was no evidence they did combine. According to the evidence if the deceased had not spoken to them, in all probability he would not have been struck by Bartley. Although the deceased might be the first to have talked about fighting, and might have thus induced Bartley to strike him, there was no justification in the eye of the law for Bartley striking him. If the deceased had assaulted Bartley, and the latter had struck him in self defence, using no more violence than was necessary to defend himself, he would have been exonerated from crime, but it did not appear that the deceased struck him, and therefore Bartley by striking him was guilty of an unlawful act, and death having ensued he was guilty of manslaughter.

After a few minutes deliberation the coroner's jury returned a verdict of manslaughter against Bartley, and he was committed for trial at Leeds Assizes.

At the assizes Bartley pleaded guilty. The judge, Mr Justice Denman, said the prisoner's position as a militiaman made the matter more disgraceful than if he had been an ordinary labourer. All four should have thought of protecting other people instead of outraging all good nature and right feeling. He would have dealt with the matter lightly if he thought the prisoner had acted out of character, but it grew out of a violent and ungovernable course, out of the habit of excess drinking and violence, resulting from brutal self indulgence. He then sentenced Bartley to penal servitude for seven years.

Thirty-Six

A BABY'S BODY IN THE VILLAGE POND

Ferrensby, 1881

The weather at the beginning of March 1881 was so cold that the village pond at Ferrensby froze over. At about noon on Thursday, 3 March 1881 Arthur Wade, the fourteen-year-old son of Robert Wade, a Ferrensby inn keeper, was breaking the ice on the pond on the wall side, when he saw a baby's foot at the top of the water. He went home but afterwards went back to look again. Satisfied he had not made a mistake he informed Robert Houseman, a stonemason, who lived close by. Houseman went to the pond and afterwards, for some undisclosed reason, went away. Young Wade lifted the body out of the water on to the wall and gave it to John Allen, a Ferrensby horse dealer. The body had been head down in about eight inches of water, and part of its face was muddy. It was naked, and there was no clothing about. Allen then took the body to Mr Wade's house.

William Renton, a Knaresborough surgeon, was called out and examined the body, which was that of a fully developed female child. Its appearance showed the mother had received no proper attention at the time of delivery. He could find no marks of violence on the body, and from its appearance would say it had been in the water many days. In his opinion the child had been born alive, but might have died naturally.

Mary Allen, wife of John Allen, said that between 8 and 9 o'clock on Tuesday night she was at home and heard what she thought was the cry of a child. She lived near the pond and could hear when anyone went to it. She heard two cries, then no more, and did not look out. She had not noticed anyone particularly about the pond that day.

At an inquest, held two days after the discovery of the body, Police Constable Thistlewood, stationed at Staveley, said he had made every possible enquiry but so far had been unable to discover the parentage of the dead child. The coroner consequently adjourned the inquest until 19 March to allow the police more time to make their inquiries.

At the adjourned inquest, held at the General Tarleton, the coroner told the jury the child might have died a natural death and then have been thrown into the pond.

The village pond, Ferrensby.

If, however, it had died from want of proper attention at the time of birth the jury would have to decide how far that neglect had been the means of causing death, and whether it would amount to the crime of murder, or manslaughter.

PC Thistlewood, and Police Sergeant Betts, said they had made diligent inquiries at various places but could obtain no evidence as to who the mother of the child might be. They had also dragged the pond where the child was found but could find no evidence. Superintendent Carr said the matter had been made as public as they could make it.

William Renton said he had carried out a post-mortem on the baby and was satisfied it had not been thrown into the water alive. The cause of death might have been continued exposure to the cold, as it was a very cold winter's night, and with no clothing on it would require only a little shock to terminate the baby's existence. That, combined with a little haemorrhage from the umbilical cord, which was left untied, would be quite sufficient to account for death.

The coroner said he did not think the evidence before them was strong enough for them to find the baby had been murdered. After some further remarks the jury returned a verdict that the child was found dead in the pond, but how it came by its death, or how it got into the water, there was not sufficient evidence to show.

The police promised not to relax their efforts and use every endeavour to try and solve the mystery, but solved it never was.

Thirty-Seven

MURDEROUS OUTRAGE ON AN OLD MAN

Felliscliffe, 1882

After being out during the day, John Davy, a seventy-seven-year-old man, who lived alone in a cottage near White Wall Lane, Felliscliffe, returned home on the evening of 18 May 1882. On entering his bedroom he was suddenly attacked by a powerful man armed with a cudgel and a stonebreaker's hammer. Although knocked down, Davy somehow managed to reach the outer door of his house (the bedroom being on the same floor) and opened it, all the time being mercilessly beaten on the head and shoulders by his attacker. On gaining the outer door Davey shouted, 'Murder!' at which his assailant ran off, leaving the cudgel in the house and throwing the stonebreaker's hammer into a hen roost in the yard. Both were later found saturated with blood. Although fearfully wounded, Davy never lost consciousness and during the night managed to reach the house of a neighbour, where he was put to bed and attended by Dr Saunders of Hampsthwaite. It was believed Davey had disturbed a burglar, it being well known in the neighbourhood that he received interest on investments due about that time. The attacker appears never to have been caught.

It is often said today that the authorities are soft on crime and that the police are rarely to be seen. These views are not new. Following the attack on Davey Joseph Hezmalhalch jnr of Holly Bank, Felliscliffe, complained that the attack on Davey would not cause any surprise. The number of prowling tramps and other vagrants who frequented the neighbourhood was such as to be a public nuisance. So long, however, as they were encouraged by certain 'would be philanthropists' it was almost useless to hope for a change. He also considered a policeman in the neighbourhood an extinct animal.

Thirty-Eight

THE ALDBOROUGH GHOST

Aldborough, 1887

Fifty years before Jack the Ripper prowled the streets of London another Jack brought terror to that city's inhabitants. This was Spring-Heeled Jack. This Jack's antics consisted mainly of jumping out on people, usually women, and breathing fire into their faces. He would then make his escape by a series of huge bounds. So high could he leap that some thought he must have springs attached to the heels of his boots, hence his name. In 1838 he made several appearances, but then faded away and was never caught. He lived on in cheap fiction, and occasionally in various parts of the country someone would frighten the local females by jumping out on them in imitation of him. This appears to have been so at Aldborough, near Boroughbridge. In October 1887 it was reported the female and timid portion of the inhabitants had been considerably scared by the appearance of what the superstitious believed to be a ghost. It appeared at the

The crossroads outside Aldborough, looking towards the village, where the 'Aldborough Ghost' would make its appearance.

dark and lonely crossroads just outside the village. The ghost wasn't brave enough to face the male population and confined its activities to sneaking out of its lair and frightening young children and females. Some said it was a person with a white sheet over his/her head. Others described it as a man dressed as a woman with a newspaper wrapped around his head, while others said it was definitely a woman. Some said it must wear spring boots, which enabled it to take amazing leaps. Ghost hunting became the favourite sport and amusement of the young men of the village, and several traps were set to catch the 'ghost,' all without success. Eventually it appeared no more, probably because some of the ghost hunters were armed with stout sticks with which to administer their own brand of justice.

Thirty-Nine

A BECKWITHSHAW WOMAN BURIED ALIVE?

Beckwithshaw, 1888

Arabella Elizabeth Tetley died of puerperal fever on 14 February 1888, shortly after giving birth. She was only twenty-three years old and the wife of William Tetley, a schoolmaster at Beckwithshaw, near Harrogate. Dr Deville of Harrogate attended her and certified the death. She was buried in Woodhouse Cemetery, Leeds, three days later, on 17 February 1888. After the funeral a story began to circulate that she had not been dead when placed in the coffin, but had been in a coma of some sorts. She had revived in the coffin and had fought to escape from the grave. The gravedigger, so the stories went, had been standing in the grave filling it with earth when he had heard knocking sounds, and felt the earth beneath his feet rise and fall slightly, as if the deceased was trying to push open the coffin lid from the inside. Somewhat concerned he had climbed out of the grave and sought out two fellow workman. The three men had then gone to the grave and stood in silence for a few minutes, listening, but had heard nothing. The other men then went about their business, and the gravedigger filled in the grave.

The story became so widespread, and the public so concerned, that Herbert Gladstone (Member of Parliament for Leeds West, and the son of former prime minister William Ewart Gladstone) raised the matter in Parliament. As a consequence, the Home Secretary ordered the body exhumed and an inquest held. The body of Mrs Tetley was therefore exhumed in the early hours of 5 March and taken to Millgarth Street Mortuary, Leeds.

On opening the inquest, the coroner, Mr J.C. Malcolm, addressed the jury:

> Gentlemen we are met to make an enquiry into the cause of death of Mrs Arabella Elizabeth Tetley. The death has already been certified by a medical man and registered, but in consequence of circumstances which have arisen, which probably you are already acquainted with, it has been become necessary to have a public examination in order that you may be able to, what I may call, re-certify as to whether the death has arisen from natural causes, or whether, unfortunately, it is a case of death from asphyxia from the woman having been put into the coffin whilst alive.

A surgeon, Mr Scattergood, with others stood, around the coffin as the lid was slowly removed. They looked inside and found the shroud, and the flowers and wreaths laid upon it, not the least disturbed. On raising the shroud Scattergood saw the hands were exactly in the position the undertaker would have placed them. There were no abrasions of any kind on them. That the body was that of Arabella Tetley was confirmed by her cousin, John Henry Radcliffe, of 20 Hanover Place, Leeds. Mrs Tetley's husband being, understandably, not up to the task of identifying it.

All eyes now turned on Fred Posey, the gravedigger, who had originated the story. He told the inquest he had dug the grave and had been present when the coffin was placed in it. The depth of the grave was about 9ft. After the mourners had departed he had shovelled in about 4 or 5ft of earth, weighing about two or three tons, and then jumped in to remove the wooden shoulder boards supporting the sides of the grave. Whilst in the grave he heard some rattling, or something like knocking. He denied he had ever said he had heard distinct knocking, or felt the upheaval of the coffin. He had been a gravedigger at Woodhouse Cemetery for five years and had not heard anything like it before. He was not frightened, but curious. He sought out two fellow workers and returned to the grave. They did not hear anything and told him it was only the cracking of the earth from the frost. He had then filled in the grave. He denied telling anyone other than his two fellow workers about the event.

Sykes Sheppard, a monumental mason employed at the cemetery, said Posey had come to him on the day of the funeral and said while filling in the grave he had heard a noise he had not heard before. He didn't seem alarmed because he lit his pipe at the fire in his (Shepherd's) shop. Shepherd, and another man, went with him to the grave but when they got there they heard nothing. It was filled up to within about 2ft 6ins of the surface. Shepherd got a spade and sounded down the side but could not hear anything at all. He simply attributed the noise Posey had heard to it being a frosty day. The rough earth went in first and the fine afterwards, and he attributed the noise to the fine earth dribbling through the rough on to the coffin lid. Shepherd said Posey

The imposing entrance to Woodhouse Cemetery.

Woodhouse Cemetery, where Mrs Tetley was not allowed to rest in peace. Most of the gravestones have been removed and the cemetery landscaped. It is now known as St George's Field.

could give him no idea when he came into the shop as to what the noise was like. Shepherd told him he thought it was nothing but superstition on his part. The three men stayed at the grave about twenty minutes and Shepherd said he tried all he knew to see if there was any further noise but could hear nothing.

The coroner told Posey the present enquires had been brought about by statements made by him (Posey) and he had caused a very serious injury to the family of the deceased woman. He added that he thought, and he thought the jury would likewise think, that he (Posey) had caused great excitement and great difficulty over nothing. There were then cries of 'hear hear.'

Addressing the jury the coroner said:

> I think, gentlemen, you have now exhausted the matter. I do not think you can do anything but return a verdict confirming Dr Deville's certificate. It is quite evident if the man has made a statement he is not making the same statement now. He says he never made the statement to the extent which has been reported. He is on his oath and you must judge. Remember that, but whatever his statement it turns out there is no foundation whatever for it.

The jury then confirmed Dr Deville's certificate and the proceedings closed. The large crowd that had gathered outside to hear the result of the inquest dispersed, and Mrs Tetley was laid to rest for the second and final time.

Forty

A MIDNIGHT HEARSE

Ripon, 1888

In the days before motor vehicles there was usually little road traffic at night. Police Constable Rogerson might therefore have been surprised to hear the sound of horses coming down the Harrogate road near Borrage Terrace, Ripon, at about half past midnight on 2 March 1888. Out of the darkness came two horses pulling a hearse, complete with a coffin in the back. The driver sat motionless on his seat. A nervous person might have run a mile, convinced it was a ghostly apparition with the corpse itself driving the hearse, but PC Rogerson was made of sterner stuff. On noticing the reins trailing on the ground he climbed aboard the hearse, and after a considerable effort managed to wake the driver. The result was that a week later Thomas Grayson

Harrogate Road looking towards Ripon and its junction with Borrage Lane. It was near this spot that PC Rogerson saw the 'Midnight Hearse'.

of Bradford appeared in court charged with driving a hearse without holding the reins, or having due control of the two horses pulling it. The hearse was travelling from Bradford to Catterick bridge. Grayson was said to have had some drink but was alright when roused. Mr Collinson, a magistrate, said it was a miserable night to be out and he would want a drink if he had a corpse under him. Grayson was nevertheless fined 1s with 9s costs, or seven days in prison if he defaulted.

Forty-One

ROBBERY WITH VIOLENCE

Ripon, 1905

On the afternoon of 12 January 1905 Thomas Rainforth, a North Eastern Railway employee for over forty years, was seated at his desk in the coal office of Ripon goods yard. It was a quiet time of day but labourers often hung about outside hoping for work in the coal yard. Five such men, Benson, Myers, Elvidge, Brown and Hardcastle, entered the office. Benson said to Rainforth, 'We've come.' When Rainforth asked, 'For what?' Benson replied, 'To sign.' When Rainforth said they had nothing to sign

Ripon railway station in the 1950s. The goods yard is on the left.

for, Benson, and one of the others, seized him by the throat and threw him to the ground. He was then held down whilst £4 6s 7d was removed from the cash drawers. Four of them then left, but Hardcastle stayed and helped Rainforth, who was almost unconscious, to his feet.

The robbers must have been exceptionally stupid because four of them were well know to Rainforth. On being informed of the robbery, Police Sergeant Wrack, and Police Constable Moore, went to the Magdalens Inn in Stonebridgegate, where the five men had spent much of the day, and had returned to celebrate their success. Benson had a reputation as a pugilist and a dangerous character, and was arrested with difficulty. He struck Police Sergeant Wrack on the jaw and both men fell struggling to the floor. At the same time Myers and Elvidge attacked PC Moore and knocked him to the ground. PC Moore, however, recovered, took out his truncheon, and knocked both men down. All the way to the police station the three men continued to fight the two policemen, so much so that PC Moore was forced to knock Myers down a second time. Myers and Elvidge apparently managed to escape, but were arrested later that day. Myers again became violent and had to be handcuffed. Brown was arrested on Ripon railway station as he waited for a train to Leeds.

The prisoners spent the night in the cells singing comic songs and next morning appeared before the magistrates. Myers had a bandaged head and Benson a scar on his cheek. All five complained of improper treatment in the police cells and asked to be remanded in Northallerton. It was not known whether they were telling the truth but their request was granted. They later appeared at Leeds Assizes. Hardcastle was sentenced to two months imprisonment, and the other four to three months.

Ripon lost its railway in 1969 as part of the Beeching cuts. However, some of the goods yard buildings still remain. This view is looking towards Ripon, with what was the main road into the city from the north now bypassed.

The Magdalens public house, Ripon, where the robbers spent much of the day and returned to celebrate their success.

Other titles published by The History Press

Hanged at Leeds
STEVE FIELDING

The history of execution at Leeds began in September 1864 when two men were hanged side by side outside the front gates. Over the next hundred years a further ninety-one men and women paid the ultimate penalty here. They include notorious cat burglar and killer Charles Peace; and two young army deserters executed for the brutal slaying of a Pontefract shopkeeper. Fully illustrated with photographs, drawings, news cuttings and rare documents, *Hanged at Leeds* will appeal to everyone interested in the shadier side of Yorkshire's history.

978 0 7509 5093 0

Infamous Yorkshire Women
ISSY SHANNON

Many remarkable women have been born in, or have strong connections with Yorkshire. In Issy Shannon's book we hear about the most infamous – including witches, thieves, fraudsters and murders. Among many other are the calculating Queen Cartimandua, ruler of the Brigantes, Mary Bateman, the Yorkshire witch, whose skin was flayed off, cut up and sold as good luck charms after her execution, and Elizabeth Broadingham, who was burned at the stake for murdering her husband in 1776.

978 0 7509 4746 6

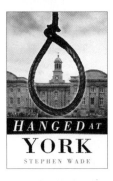

Hanged at York
STEPHEN WADE

Hanged at York gathers together the stories of criminals hanged at York from the middle of the eighteenth century to the late nineteenth century. The condemned featured here ranged from coiners and forgers to murderers, thieves and highwaymen, the most infamous being Dick Turpin, who was hanged on Yorks Knavesmire in 1739 for horse-stealing. Stephen Wades' highly readable new book is fully illustrated with photographs, news cuttings and engravings.

978 0 7509 5042 8

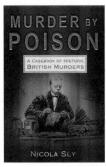

Murder by Poison: A Casebook of Historic British Murders
NICOLA SLY

Readily obtainable and almost undetectable prior to advances in forensic science during the twentieth century, poison was considered the ideal method of murder and many of its exponents failed to stop at just one victim. Along with the most notorious cases of murder by poison in the country, such as those of Mary Ann Cotton and Dr Thomas Neil Cream, this book also features many of the cases that did not make national headlines, examining not only the methods and motives but also the real stories of the perpetrators and their victims.

978 0 7524 5065 0

Visit our website and discover thousands of other History Press books.

www.thehistorypress.co.uk

The History Press